Doctor James W. Nicholson

STORIES OF DIXIE
by
James W. Nicholson, A.M. LL.D
Professor of Mathematics
Louisiana State University

With Illustrations

THE CONFEDERATE
REPRINT COMPANY
☆   ☆   ☆   ☆
WWW.CONFEDERATEREPRINT.COM

Stories of Dixie
by James W. Nicholson

Originally Published in 1915
by American Book Company
New York

Reprint Edition © 2015
The Confederate Reprint Company
Post Office Box 2027
Toccoa, Georgia 30577
www.confederatereprint.com

Cover and Interior by
Magnolia Graphic Design
www.magnoliagraphicdesign.com

ISBN-13: 978-0692461303
ISBN-10: 0692461302

DEDICATION

One of the wisest and most beautiful acts related in this book is that referred to by Governor McEnery in the conclusion of the story of the Gee Place: "When Doctor Egan and my father died their sons came together and agreed not to prolong the feud of their fathers. Accordingly, the matter was dropped and forgotten, and there are now no warmer friends in the State than the sons of those two good men."

The Children of Those Who Wore the Blue

and

The Children of Those Who Wore the Gray,

in pursuing the same wise and patriotic course,
have given to the nation's history its most glorious chapter.

To these sons and daughters, North and South,
this little labor of love is dedicated.

PREFACE

    This book is made up of true stories about Dixie – stories of people and conditions. In it there are no excesses and no fanciful creations, whether of persons or affairs. Its aim is to instruct and entertain by portraying, simply and truthfully, real things and happenings in Dixie.

    If the history of the South be regarded as a building, this book aims to be the vestibule thereof, and the attempt has been made so to construct and furnish it that those who enter therein may be incited to go on into the building itself. Should it be thought that too much is said of trifles the reply would be: (1) the book is intended mainly for young people; and (2) one has a lop-sided knowledge of the people of Dixie who knows nothing of their jokes and sports.

    A quasi biography of "Nick" runs through the book. While true, as far as it goes, its purpose is chiefly mechanical. It is somewhat of a path winding its way through a forest from which the necessary bearings are taken to draw a map of the tract. Around it are woven the "stories of Dixie" pretty much as the gems and jewels of a crown are entwined about the skeleton frame that holds them in order, continuity, and perspective.

    The White people of the South are generally homogeneous as to manners, habits, and ideals. They sprang from a common ancestry and have been molded by like means and agencies. Probably the section which was most representative of the whole South in 1860 was North Louisiana. At that time it was the last section settled, and its healthful climate, fertile lands, and abundant timber, fish, and game attracted settlers from all parts of the South. It was Dixie in a nutshell, and for this reason it is made the scene of many of the stories.

This book had its origin in two suggestions, one coming from a Northern and the other from a Southern source:

In the early spring of 1913 the author, while dining with Dr. W. T. H. Howe, of Cincinnati, Ohio, attempted to entertain him with stories of the South. The doctor's appreciation of the narratives was such that he suggested the writing and publishing of them in book form.

About the same time *The Daily Picayune,* of New Orleans, having referred very approvingly to a communication from Dr. Van Dyke to the children of New Jersey, suggested a message from the present writer to the children of Louisiana.

The author wishes to thank most heartily his colleague Hugh Mercer Blain, Ph.D., Professor of English, who has read the manuscript and offered many helpful suggestions.

In retraveling, as it were, the long voyage described in this book the author has been accompanied by his daughter, Mrs. A. P. Daspit, and to him she has been a cheering and helpful companion, – a motor and a rudder. Among other things she has often reminded him of the two old maxims: "The secret of being tiresome is in telling everything," and "The most completely lost of all days is that on which one has not laughed."

CONTENTS

CHAPTER ONE
The Story of a Typical Settler

Cane Ridge 13
Events and Stories 18
Good Dogs, a Coon Hunt, and a Fight 20
Nick and the Cardinal 23
An Old-Time School 25
A Hunt, a Whir, a Rustle, and a Stampede 28

CHAPTER TWO
The Atlantic Slope

Growth of the Colonies 35
The Call of the West 37
The Westward Movement 39
An Illustration of the Westward Movement 41

CHAPTER THREE
The Story of a Westward Move

More "Elbow Room" 45
Off For Louisiana 46
New Orleans Then and Now 48
Up the Red River 52

CHAPTER FOUR
The Story of a Typical Neighborhood

Uncle Wash Moves From Cane Ridge 61
Progressive Development 64
The Forest Grove School 70

CHAPTER FIVE
The Story of a Typical Section

Typical of Dixie	75
Two Good Signs	76
The Gee Place	76
A Peaceful and Prosperous Land	81
Religion and Churches	82
Introducing Oat	85
Homer College	87

CHAPTER SIX
The Story of the Beginnings of the War

The Irrepressible Conflict	93
Nick Goes to War	94
Camp Moore	100

CHAPTER SEVEN
The Story of Events of the War

Minor Incidents	107
A Fish Story	110
A Confederate Scout	112
Stories of Oat	114
An Interrupted Oration	117
The Confederate Army Starts For Tennessee	122
A Student Soldier	124
A Perilous Adventure	126
General Sherman and Colonel Boyd	128

CHAPTER EIGHT
The Story of the Close of the War

Cheerful Endurance	133
Closing Scenes	134
The Fortunes of an Old Flag	137
The Curtain Falls on a Scene Both Sad and Droll	139

CHAPTER NINE
The Story of the Homeward Tramp

The Remnant Starts Home 143
A Great Southern Leader 144
An Old-Time Southern Aristocrat 145
A Few Great Georgians 149
A Long and Jolly Ride 153
More Surprises 156
The Gulf and Its Chief Tributary 158
The Home Stretch 161

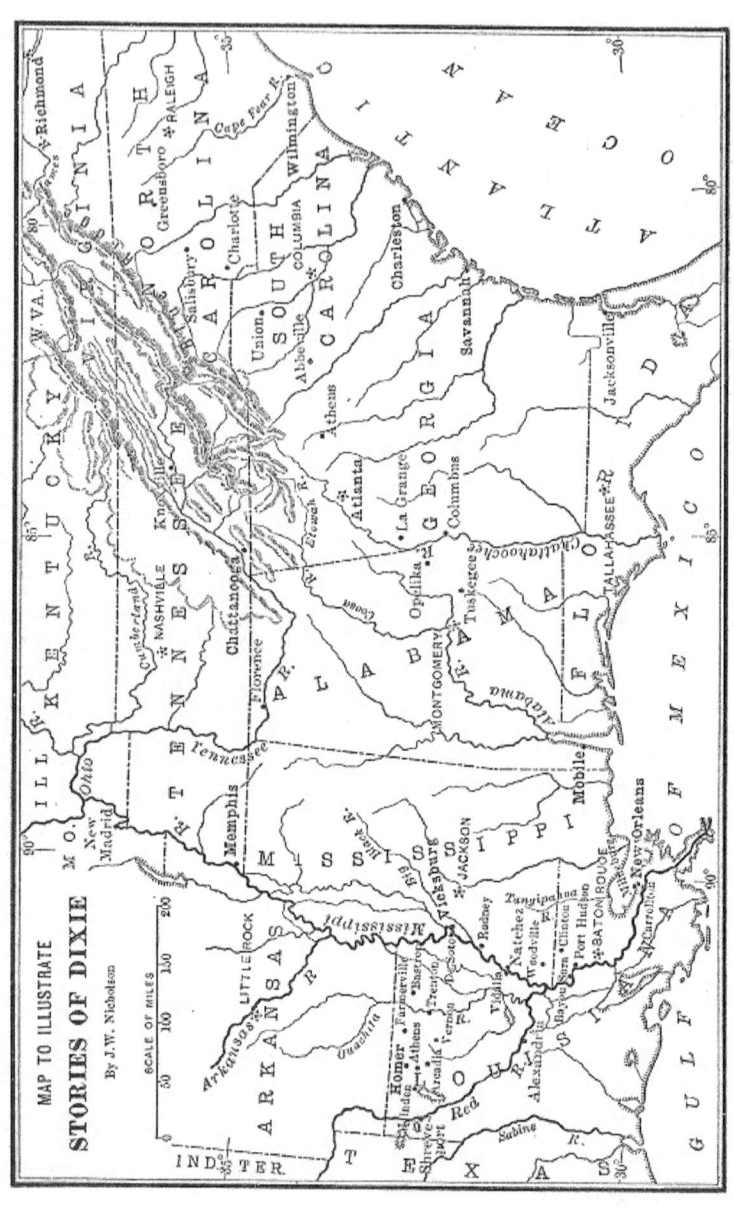

CHAPTER ONE
The Story of a Typical Settler

Cane Ridge

A long time ago four sturdy oxen were drawing a heavy wagon through the valleys and over the hills of northern Louisiana. There was, here and there, the semblance of a road winding its way through the forest and connecting the crude homes of the settlers who had entered these wilds and broken their long silence with the ax and the gun. Uncle Nathan, driver of the team, often found it necessary to stop and remove a log or tree top from the path, or cut a way around a deep and rugged washout.

Never did one look upon a lovelier land; at least, so thought Uncle Wash, who rode on horseback ahead of his wagon to select the best route and lead Uncle Nathan along the way of least resistance. To him a charming feature of the country was that it was so little defaced and defiled by man's habitation. There was a profusion of wild flowers, great and splendid trees, and rich valleys separated by gentle swells which now and then rose to the dignity of hills. Springs of clear, pure water spouted from the hillsides, and numerous brooks, fed from these fountain heads, ran down the valleys and flowed with a cheerful murmur through the land. Along the creeks, formed by the joining of these branches, were numerous swamps varying in width from a few rods to half a mile.

To one who has no great love of the wilds these swamps would have had a dismal aspect, owing to to their murky bayous, the dark shadows of the luxuriant woods, and the rank growths of vines and cane. Not so with Uncle Wash. Even the gaunt cypress knees, which stood like ghosts in the muddy lowlands, were as attractive to him as the graceful pines on the hills or the white dogwood blossoms in the valleys.

Two years before the scene here described Uncle Wash had moved from Alabama to Louisiana. On reaching this new, and to him unknown, land he thought best to select a temporary site, and prepare hasty quarters in which he and his might live until he could look about and find a choice locality for his permanent home. This had been done, and he was now moving from the first place to the site of the second one. The party consisted of himself, Aunt Martha (his wife), his little children, and a few slaves, among whom were Uncle Nathan and Aunt Kitty (the cook). Late one summer afternoon the movers arrived at the point where their new home was to be established.

In the center of the new locality was a hill of medium size, crowned by a flat tract of about six acres. The east side of the hill sloped down to a clear branch that flowed at its base; the west side dipped down more abruptly to a rich plateau that extended to a pretty stream called Cane Creek; and the north and south sides slanted down more gently to rich valleys. It was a wild and romantic-looking place. On the hill and in the valleys were great trees – oak, ash, hickory, elm, pine, beech, gum – and in the swamps grew many cypresses; in the midst of all were growths of ironwood, dogwood, maple, chinquapin, holly and witch-hazel. Here and there were networks of grape and muscadine vines so dense that the sun seldom shone through them. Large reed-canes covered the valleys, and a smaller kind, called switch-cane, extended far up the hillsides.

Having reached the end of their rough journey, the movers dismounted and began hasty preparations for the night. While the men were feeding the stock and providing temporary quarters, the women were busy cooking the evening meal. Although only hoe-cake, fried venison, and coffee formed this frugal repast, yet seldom has a more elegant and bountiful one been so thoroughly enjoyed. As slice after slice of the meat was fried, the savory odor caused all to realize how hungry they were. What a stimulus to hearty eating is life in the woods!

The next morning Uncle Wash stood on the hill, viewed the prospect, and formed his plans. "I will build my houses," said he, "on the top of this hill, where my family and Negroes will be above the malaria of the lowlands; I will build my barns, horse-lot, and cowpen on the gentle slope by the branch, where the stock will always have plenty of water; I will plant my garden on the rich plateau at the foot of the hill on the other side; and I will have my fields in the fertile valleys on the north and south sides."

There was much hard work to be done. Houses were to be built, lands cleared, rails split, and fences made; and many other things of more or less importance had to be attended to. Among the most urgent of the many needs were houses to live in. So the building of cabins was at once begun. There being no lumber mills in the country, these dwellings were made of the halves of round pine logs, notched at the ends so that they would lie close together. The small cracks between the pieces were lined on the inside with boards and chinked on the outside with a kind of mortar made of clay and straw.

At least a part of these huts was first-class, and that was the roof. Cypress trees were plentiful. A choice one was selected, felled, and sawed into short cuts. From these cuts the sapwood was removed and the remaining heartwood split into bolts, which were rived into boards by means of a froe. The cabins were covered with these boards. A roof so made has been known to last "three score years and ten."

The next work of importance was opening and fencing the fields, and putting them in a state of tillage. Where a wilderness of goodly trees had overspread the ground there was soon naught but blackened stumps, and along the wooded border of the bright sunny opening was a strong worm fence ten rails high. With the plowing of the land came the blackbird and the bluebird, whose merry chirping seemed to be attuned to the bracing odor of the fresh upturned soil.

On the farm and garden and about the house and yard there was something for every one to do. Men, women, and children, White and Black, worked from dawn to dark. It was a hive in which there were no drones. All hands arose in the morning, as Uncle Wash ordered, "by times."

Breakfast and supper were prepared and eaten by the light of a "suet lamp." This old-time lamp is entitled to more than a passing notice. The only means the settlers had of obtaining lights were with pine knots, lightwood, and grease. The kind of grease most used by the pioneers was a crude oil taken from the fat of bears. A saucer or tin plate was filled with the grease, and into it was dropped a cord with one end protruding. The exposed end was lighted, and served as the wick of a candle. This outfit, often called a suet lamp, being better than anything of the kind the settlers had ever seen, was thought by them to "just fill the bill."

When beef tallow and mutton suet became more plentiful than bear's oil, one of these was used instead of the latter. In the march of progress the suet lamp was followed by "molded tallow" candles, and these by "store-bought star" candles, which, in time, gave place to coal oil lamps. The latter came into use in that section soon after the close of the Civil War.

A smokehouse was a necessary part of every settler's home. In it meat of all kinds was cured and kept. It had no floor. On the "dirt floor," as it was called, a fire was made and kept burning day and night, but it was so smothered that it burned slowly, producing little fire and much smoke. The smoke cured the meat, and I doubt whether there has ever been any way of making sweeter meat. If you have never eaten smoked bacon or sausage you have missed, according to Uncle Nathan, "de nex bes' thing to possum and taters."

A great deal of salt was wasted in curing meat, and this was absorbed by the dirt floor on which it fell. Thus, in the course of years, this ground became a very good salt mine. During the Civil War, when salt became scarce, many Southern families dug up the ground floors of their old smokehouses and obtained enough salt from the dirt to tide them over the hour of need. This was an instance in which waste proved to be "bread cast upon the waters."

As soon as Uncle Wash had the time and means he built larger and more comfortable houses. In front of the cabin occupied by the Whites he erected a very creditable residence, and the cabin thus vacated was fitted up for a kitchen and dining room.

In the course of time other settlers came, and with this growth in population and means the roads were improved and the streams bridged. After a while the towns of Homer and Farmerville, the county seats of two adjoining parishes, were founded. Uncle Wash helped to plan and make the road joining these towns.

It ran by his home, and when a mail route was put on it a post office was located in his house. For this office he suggested the name of Cane Ridge, and it still goes by that name.

Events and Stories

Uncle Wash had the gifts and arts of a good woodssportsman. He was a tireless walker and sat a horse as if he were a part of it. With an innate love of trapping and fowling, fishing and hunting, few surpassed him in the use of the gun and the fishing rod, and fewer still in the art of making and setting traps and nets. He was divided between love of fields and love of swamps, with the greater inclination toward swamps. The prospects of abundant crops and abundant sports were equally well pleasing to him.

As to manner and matter the following is typical of conversations held at Cane Ridge:

"My dear," said Aunt Martha to Uncle Wash, "the meat is about out, and you will have to take your gun and obtain some from the woods."

"Can't do it, Martha; can't do it. Too busy now," said he.

Uncle Wash liked to be urged to do the very thing he most desired to do, especially to hunt. He wished people to think that he never neglected his duties on the farm for the pleasures and spoils of the woods. But he did not fool Aunt Martha; she knew he was always anxious to get into the woods with his gun and dogs.

However, she never seemed to doubt his sincerity. So now she said, "I know you are quite busy, my dear, but neither you nor the hands can work very long without something to eat."

"The hands," said he, "are now doing a certain work, and if I leave them they will either do it wrong or not do it at all. Really you had better feed us all on scraps to-morrow."

He took his hat and started toward the door. But, seeing that Aunt Martha was not going to urge him further, he stopped and said, "It has just occurred to me, Martha, that I have to go in the woods soon to select some rail timber, and by going now I might kill two birds with the same stone. What kind of game do you wish, large or small?"

"As you wish to get back to your work as soon as possible, we can make out with a few birds or squirrels; and these you can get near by."

"While I am at it," said he, "I might just as well get enough to last some time."

He went, and in a few hours returned for Nathan; he needed him to help bring home probably a deer and a gobbler.

In the course of time Uncle Wash had a number of cows and hogs, and they throve on the rich food they obtained in the range. The cows were milked in the cowpen by Aunt Kitty, and there was enough butter, buttermilk or "clabber" to supply both Whites and Blacks. Just before "hog-killing time" the hogs were "stall-fed"; that is, they were penned and fed on corn. This made the meat sweet.

As night came on the stock would leave the woods, come home, and sleep under the trees around the yard. Even some of the hogs which had become wild in the woods would do this to protect themselves and their young ones from the wolves and bears. Some animals seem to show great foresight in this way. A mother deer will leave her young fawn in the bushes near a public road, knowing that bears and wolves are not likely to go near where men travel.

One day Uncle Wash went into the woods to

look after some of his wild hogs. Just as he reached a bend in the path along which he was riding he met a panther. The beast was not more than twenty feet away. It at once crouched and began to wag its tail, which is the habit of the panther when about to spring on its prey. Uncle Wash usually went well armed, but at this time he had only his great bowie knife. He knew that with this he could cleave the animal's head if he got a fair chance, but he did not wish to run the risk of getting such a chance.

Wild animals seldom attack a man except when driven to it by hunger or in self-defense. As a rule they are more afraid of a man than he is of them. Uncle Wash knew this, and adopted the hunter's method of cowering the beast by out-staring it. With his knife in his hand he and the panther gazed mutely but intently into each other's eyes. Finally the animal glanced to one side as if looking for a safe place of retreat; then the rider suddenly spurred his horse and it leaped toward the panther. This so frightened the wild beast that it scampered off into the woods as fast as it could go.

Good Dogs, A Coon Hunt, and a Fight

Uncle Wash was fond of dogs, and all dogs liked him on a very short acquaintance. He would walk boldly into a yard, seemingly not noticing the fierce dogs that threatened to attack him, and right in the face of the angry animals he would squat down quietly and in a low and jovial tone say: "Howdy do, boys! How are you all to-day? Come up and let's talk it over." At first they looked at him as if they thought he was crazy; but soon they were his friends. One of his sayings was, "You can always tie to the man that loves a dog."

The Story of a Typical Settler

Every stray dog in the "regions around" would come to him, and he was never known to turn one away. However poor and no-account the dog was on its arrival, it was soon changed into a fat, useful, and "genteel" dog. Uncle Wash was never without a number of good dogs – hunting dogs and watchdogs. The barking of these faithful sentinels at night gave everyone, even the cows and hogs, a feeling of safety. It is mostly in pioneer life that one comes to love and value a good dog.

Early one morning, Uncle Wash and Uncle Nathan went into the fields to kill some coons that were destroying the young corn growing near the swamps. Uncle Wash took his gun and Uncle Nathan his ax.

"Now, Nathan," said Uncle Wash, "the only dogs we need are Rouse, Bull, and Step."

The first two were large and strong and the third was an active heavy-built fice. All were stalwart and valiant, and eager for a fray with a coon or a panther. Rouse, especially, was the hero of many a well-fought battle.

They came to a point in the field where there was a dense canebrake just outside. The dogs roused something and chased it off through the canebrake. "That is no coon or bear," said Uncle Wash. "It is a wildcat, a catamount, or a panther."

It is strange how an old hunter can tell from the way his dogs chase an animal what kind of animal it is. In a short time the yelping of the dogs was changed to a deep-mouthed baying. "They have treed it," said Uncle Wash, "and we must go to them at once."

They climbed over the fence and plunged into the canebrake. Uncle Nathan went ahead, and bent or cut the cane so that they could pass through. At last they came to an open glade, in the center of which was a large hollow cypress log, and in this the beast had taken refuge. Step was staring into the hollow log

and growling. The hair on his back stood straight up, and he had braced himself as if for a battle. Uncle Wash patted him on the back and said, "Sick 'em, boy," and into the log Step went. There was at once the rumble of a severe tussle – gnashing, biting, and scratching. Poor Step! He soon came out, and with gashes on his head and neck he looked up sadly into his master's face and seemed to say: "I can't whip him by myself."

"I thought so," said Uncle Wash, "it is a catamount."

Now a catamount is like a wildcat, but much larger, stronger, and fiercer. Nathan then cut a hole in the top of the log, and it happened to be just over the animal's neck. Uncle Wash, hoping to have some fun, cut a forked stick, straddled it over the beast, and threw his weight upon it. But the cat was so strong it slipped from under the stick and came boldly out of the log. Step nabbed it first, probably knowing that he was not now to fight the battle alone.

In an instant Rouse and Bull flew to Step's aid, and the fight was on. Round and round, over and over they went, growling and biting, scratching and gnashing. The great cat slashed with its long claws and bit with its sharp teeth, rending the hides and tearing the flesh of the dogs. But the dogs had strong jaws and long teeth, a courage that knew no fear, and nerves that would stand all pain. They gave a bite for a scratch and a gash for every wound. At last the cat, getting a good chance, leaped again into the hollow log.

Now the cat might have been killed with the gun or the ax; but Uncle Wash, like all sportsmen, preferred to see "the fight to a finish." So he told old Nathan to split open the old shell. This done, the cat made a great leap to a near-by tree, but before it could ascend, the dogs seized it and dragged it to the ground. The fight was renewed with vigor and ferocity. Rouse fought to reach the cat's neck and the cat fought to defend it. Rouse won, seized the vital spot, and sank his teeth deep into the cat's throat. That was the last of the fight.

Nick and the Cardinal

Nowhere are birds more numerous or more beautiful than in Louisiana, and nowhere are their notes richer or their songs sweeter. Many of them come every springtime as old friends returning from rambles in foreign lands, and many others here live and die, – helpful and cheering neighbors no less in December than in May. Among these latter is the redbird, or cardinal. Perched on a twig in the garden it is easily mistaken for a brilliant poinsettia. Alert and erect, graceful and strong, with its martial notes resembling those of a fife, it is fittingly known as the cardinal. In no other small creature are the lines of strength and beauty more elegantly blended. It is a friend to the farmer and an ornament to the field and forest, and its destruction should be prevented by custom as well as by law. It would seem that no one would wish to destroy a thing so pretty, so harmless, and so useful. But consideration for a bird from a boy! One might as well look for mercy in a pack of hounds pursuing a fox.

Nick was no exceptional boy. He had seen his father (Uncle Wash) make coops and traps and catch quails and turkeys in them. So when he was seven years old he made a trap without

Nick when a little boy

any help, and set it in a brier patch where many small birds were in the habit of going everyday. One morning, going quietly to it, he peeped over the weeds and, oh! – there redbird in it. His heart beat for joy. He slipped his hand under the trap and seized the bird. Maybe he did not know that a cardinal can bite, and bite hard; but he soon found it out. When he caught the bird it seized his finger with its strong bill. But one thing sure, Nick was not going to let the bird go. He thought too much of the cardinal for that. With his left hand he pulled the bird loose from the other hand. Now the cardinal, plucky soldier that he is, resolved that if he must die he would die fighting. As fast as Nick pulled him loose from one hand he grabbed the other. This grabbing and pulling went on so fast it looked as if Nick was pulling candy. At last the boy got the cardinal by the head and clutched it so hard that, as Nick said, "the mouth could not come open." The blood was oozing from the scratches on Nick's fingers, and when he reached home his hands and the cardinal were pretty much of the same color.

An Old-Time School

For a long time there was no school or church near Cane Ridge. In the course of time the settlers thought there were enough of them to erect a building that would answer for both a church and a school. The spot chosen for it was about one mile east of Cane Ridge. The house was made of round pine logs, and the pulpit and floor of heavy slabs hewn with a broadax. There was a wide slab of the same kind fastened to the walls, all around, to answer the purpose of desks, on which the pupils were taught to write, using pens made of goose quills. The seats were the halves of round logs with four pegs for legs, the flat side forming the top. There were no desks or blackboards.

When Nick started to this school, a man having a squint, whom the boys called "Cross-eyed Bill," was the teacher. Speaking of the course of study a wag said, "It is made up of spelling, reading, writing, ciphering, and flogging." Cross-eyed Bill always kept on hand a good supply of switches – chinquapin for the girls and hickory for the boys. The patrons measured the merits of the school very largely by the number of boys and girls that got "licked" every day. One night when Dick Williams reached home his father asked, "Dick, how many uv em got licked to-day?"

"Jes three boys and two gals," said Dick.

"'Twon't do," said the old man, "'twon't do; de dis'pline of de school is givin' way; de Board will have to look into it."

Among the textbooks used were Webster's blue-back speller and Smiley's arithmetic. One of the "practical" subjects of the latter was "Barter and Trade." A problem like the following was thought to be very practical: A farmer bought 500 yards of cottonade at 5¼ cents a yard and agreed to pay for it with fox hides at $2.50 per hide; how many hides did it take? Another noted section of arithmetic was the "Rule of Three." It was commonly believed that any "sum" (problem) could be "worked" (solved) by this this rule, yet scarcely one in a hundred could solve anything by it. One of the patrons said, "I would never let a son of mine go beyond the rule of three, for I have never seen a boy do so that did not take the big head."

Near the door was a bucket of water, and above it hung a gourd dipper. Standing in the doorway and pretending to drink water gave the students a chance and an excuse to get a good view of anyone passing along the public road, a sight that was sought as one of unfailing interest. Hence, the sound of an approaching horse, buggy, or wagon was the pretext for a number of boys and girls to become very thirsty and rush for the bucket.

Of all the problems the boys had to solve none gave them more concern than trying to "cipher out" when Cross-eyed Bill was looking at them. You see, one of his eyes looked one way and the other another way, and many a poor boy got into trouble by looking at the wrong eye.

Most of the boys prided themselves in being good spitters. They had a way of spitting between two fingers pressed against their lips. The targets on which they practiced and exploited their skill were flies crawling on the floor, and at a range of six feet or less they were pretty "sho' shots." One day Clay Harper said to his mother, "Ma, Nick can't spell much, but he sho' can cipher and spit."

The signal for "taking in school" was a series of loud blows with a heavy stick on the shutter of a door or window; and for "turning out school" the master simply said, "Dismissed." When the school was dismissed for the dinner recess, the students seized their buckets, bottles, and baskets and rushed for the campus. On hot summer days they usually took their places in groups

under shady trees, some sitting on logs and others half reclining on the grass or leaves. Without any regard for rules or ceremony, they at once began to respond to the demands of hunger, each family eating its own food. At first it was much eating and little talking, but as the dinner progressed there was less of the first and more of the other.

These children of the woods had had but little training in the niceties of cultured life, yet in morals and manners they had a code which was not without merit. For instance, while one of them was talking the others were quiet and attentive. They were quick to see the funny side of a situation, and therefore, as a rule, enjoyed a joke whether they were the jokers or the joked. Their jokes, stories, and sallies of wit were mostly of personal events, of which the following are fair samples:

The boys, with few exceptions, went barefooted. On one occasion John T. was lying on his back with his bare feet resting on a log. "John," said one of the boys, "you have the longest heels of any boy I ever saw." "Why," said another, "the most of his foot is behind." "Yes," drawled John, "I was nearly two years old before they all knew which way I was going to walk."

Henry S. was known as a "big eater," and he gloried in the distinction. After "cleaning out" his basket, about which the boys were joking him, he told this story on himself: "I went to a barbecue the other day, and they had a mighty sight of good grub; I won't say how much I et, but this I will say, when I mounted old Bedford to go home he kicked up with me because he thought he was toting double."

Miss Josephine M. was a small and somewhat deformed old-young lady. She was very bright and quite thorough in all her studies except arithmetic. "Miss Joe," said her friend Tom, "I have often wondered what caused you to be bent and twisted up as you are," referring to her deformities. "Well, I don't mind telling you," said she; "I got tangled up this way studying fractions in arithmetic."

However, it ill becomes one nowadays to speak lightly of, or undervalue that old-time school. With all its follies and excesses it had its good points and served its day and time in some useful ways. In any event, we should not kick the cradle that rocked us in our infancy, although we may decline to lie in it again.

A Hunt, a Whir, a Rustle and a Stampede

Uncle Wash and Uncle Nathan went out early one morning to hunt for a wild turkey. They reached the swamp just before daybreak, the hour when all the woods are still. It was the lull between the night and the day's toils and songs. The owl had hushed its hooting, the frog its croaking, and the whippoorwill its plaintive piping, while the sparrow, the lark and the bluejay had not yet begun their morning carols. A little while since, myriads of insects were dronning, and soon as many more would raise their humming chorus. This, the darkest hour of the night, is, in the woods, the calmest of the twenty-four.

On this occasion the silence was broken only by a gobbler who was making the welkin ring by his peculiar song, if song it be. It is probably so called by those who like *Turkish* music! The hunters approached the gobbler cautiously, and stopped a hundred yards or so from its position.

"Now, Nathan," said Uncle Wash, "you squat down here in the cane and bushes, and go to yelping as clearly, smoothly, and loudly as you can; I will go some distance towards the turkey, hide myself, and await his coming."

But Uncle Nathan was scary and had a great horror of being stationed in such a dark and dismal place all by himself, knowing, too, that bears and other fierce beasts prowled in the swamp.

"Marse Wash," said he, "might'n I go long wi' you and do de yelpin'?"

"Look here, Nathan," Uncle Wash, "if you are to be scared we might as well quit right now, for no excited man can do good yelping. A turkey is the hardest thing in the woods to fool, and he will detect the least tremor or false note in your yelping, and fly away at once. I shall be only a few steps off, and nothing is going to hurt you."

They took their positions; Uncle Nathan began to yelp nicely; the gobbler drew nearer; and everything promised well, except for the turkey. But "the best laid schemes 'o mice an' men gang aft a-gley." As often happens, the unexpected occurred. In a very short time the stillness of the woods was changed into an uproar. It all came about by another party, on a similar mission, entering upon the scene. A wildcat, likewise in pursuit of food, was prowling in these woods, and hearing what he took to be the yelping of a turkey, he turned his attention and his activities in that direction. If you have ever seen a house cat creep up on a bird, you have some idea of the stealthy and crafty manner in which the great woods cat advanced upon poor Uncle Nathan.

Having gone as near to its victim as it pleased, the active beast leaped into the cane that screened the yelper, lit on Uncle Nathan, and began some surgical operations on his back. It did not take Uncle Nathan long to get busy. The first act of his performance was to give a yell that would have done credit to a Cherokee Indian. The Negro and the cat at once saw their mistakes – the one in coaxing and the other in assaulting the wrong kind of turkey. Both were surprised and terrified, and, as soon as they could untangle themselves, they began to part company.

Three distinct commotions followed Uncle Nathan's yell. The first was a whir up through the air; this was made by the gobbler as he winged his flight to parts unknown. The second was a rustle down through the swamp towards a canebrake; that was made by the cat. The third was a stampede up through the swamp in the direction of the house; this was made by Uncle Nathan. Uncle Wash, having heard the yell and the commotion, and being an old hunter, at once took in the situation, and having a keen sense of humor he laughed almost as loud as the other uncle had yelled. He lost the gobbler, it is true, but was fully recompensed by the joy he got out of the whir, the rustle, and the stampede.

There is no record as to how fast the cat ran. It must have done the best it could, for it was not only frightened but probably ashamed that it should have mistaken a darky for a turkey. As for Uncle Nathan – well, all he lacked of flying was that he now and then touched the ground with the fore-ends of his feet. It was the one time that he did no grumbling or wailing, the energy necessary to do these was put into his legs and feet. These were his main dependence.

Of course he "trusted in de Lawd," but he did not let his legs and feet know that he was so trusting. In this long stampede he made but one exclamation. Scaring up a rabbit he is reported to have said, "Git out de way, rabbit, and let a man run what kin run."

Some time after that Uncle Wash jokingly said, "Nathan, would you like to go in the woods tomorrow morning and yelp up a gobbler for me?"

"Mars Wash," said he, "I done thro'd dat yelper 'way. S'pose you git Alf; he's er mulater nigger, an' don't look so much like a wile turkey as a Black feller like me."

We shall see more of this faithful old servant in the pages which follow. Suffice it here to say, he was trusty in all undertakings except such as exposed him to personal danger.

The subsequent careers of Uncle Wash and Nick will be related after the reader has been informed somewhat of the origin and movements of their ancestors. It will be interesting and instructive to know where these typical settlers came from, and the causes and incentives which brought them into the wilds of Louisiana. So the next two chapters will give a brief account of the landing of the first English pioneers on the Atlantic Coast, and how they pushed their way westward through the wilderness, opening lands, founding homes, and building up this great nation. After that the story of Nick will be resumed, touching on his experiences in the woods and on the farm, at college and in the Civil War.

CHAPTER TWO
The Story of the Pioneers
☆ ☆ ☆ ☆

The Atlantic Slope

The Atlantic Slope is, in the main, the land which is drained by the streams that flow into the Atlantic Ocean. Starting at the mouth of one of the larger of these streams, and following it up, one would get higher and higher and finally reach the Allegheny Mountains, or one of their numerous spurs. Before the White people came from the "old world" to live in the "new world," this slope was inhabited by Indians and wild beasts.

On April 26, 1607, Captain John Smith, with a party coming over to live in the new world, reached that part of the Atlantic Slope which is called Virginia. It was a goodly land, fertile and charmful. Seldom did the landscape need distance to give enchantment to the view. The hills and valleys followed one another in such regular and graceful undulations that they were not unlike the stately swells and heaves of the ocean after the violence of the storm is spent. The Blue Ridge has many tireless rivals for man's admiration. Of these are the distant hills with their varying tints and the lovely valleys with their carpets of green. The lark soars high in the blue arch overhead, pours forth its notes of joy, and seems to say, "The world is full of brightness, of sweetness, and of hope."

April 26, 1607, may be remembered as the date of the first permanent English settlement in America. Few persons stop to think of the courage and heroism of these English settlers. Nowadays men and women cross the Atlantic in a few days, making the voyage in elegant and well furnished steamers, and give scarce a thought to the hazard of it. Then it was a journey of many weeks, in frail vessels and into unknown conditions of land and water. This was the situation faced by Captain Smith and his followers. Besides the visible perils, there were untold dangers of which they knew naught. Worn by the travails of a long sea voyage, they began life in the woods – a wilderness so vast that no man could say where it had its beginning and where its ending. Within the range of eye or ear there were no signs of man's abode, no wisps of smoke to mark the place of hut or tenement, no sound of bell, no bleat of sheep, nor distant crow of chanticleer to cheer the deep twilight calm. With the approach of darkness came a jumble of night sounds – hoots of owls, calls of whippoorwills, and chantings of katydids – and against the blackness of the woods flashed the fitful lights of countless fireflies.

But the settlers were brave and industrious. They built

rough cabins to live in, and opened small fields and gardens in which they raised corn and vegetables. In the course of time more White people came to live in this new world, building their homes near the places where they landed. Thus was formed a strip of settlements all along the Atlantic coast from Georgia to Maine. With the increase in population this strip became wider and wider, extending up the Atlantic Slope and pushing the Indians and wild beasts further back into the interior. The settlers met with many difficulties and suffered many hardships. They were often at war with the Indians, and many of them died of disease, exposure, and want of proper care or food. But toils, failures, and misfortunes called forth new effort; the greater the labor they undertook the greater always their spirit. It was as if they said, "The Atlantic Slope will never be abandoned by men of English descent; they have come to claim it, and here will they abide to found a new nation."

Growth of the Colonies

From 1607 to 1787 the number of the settlers increased from one hundred and five persons to about three million. This increase in population during these one hundred and eighty years, however great, was not so striking as the growth of the colonies in other ways. Agriculture and the industries throve, and trade and commerce increased. Very good roads and bridges were constructed, schools and colleges founded, fine churches and residences erected, and systems of county and State governments organized.

The colonists enjoyed largely the blessings of civil country life. Under such conditions what a wonderful healer and teacher is the woods! Pure air, wholesome exercise, and plenty of refreshing sleep are its tonics, and freedom, nature, and harmonies are its lessons. There is rest in its quietude, cheer in its songs, and inspiration in its scenes and activities.

While lacking in the accomplishments of life, country people are, as a rule, lusty and stalwart, muscular and manly, and brimful of good will and hospitality. "They are much like others," says Mr. Comstock, "only they have the rough bark on. They are a great deal more vital – the bark has, somehow, kept the sap richer. The polishing takes something away." "Every large city," says Dr. Eliot, "is a consuming fire in which the human race would burn itself out in a few generations were it not for the fresh blood it receives from the country."

Born and reared in the freedom of the air and the woods, enjoying the rights of life, liberty, and the pursuit of happiness, country people have always been among the first to resist the sway of tyrants. While their love of liberty and independence sometimes runs counter to the wholesome restraints of civilization, it is well to remember that republics have had their births in the country, and ceased to be democracies when they lost the spirit and lessons of the woods. How natural that a great republic should have sprung up in the free wilds of America. The pioneers who invaded these vast solitudes, cleared the lands and tilled the soil, imbibed the spirit of liberty and the ideals of freedom from all their environments, and it was only a question of time when they would no longer endure the yoke of the kingdoms beyond the seas. In this spirit of liberty and these ideals of freedom the colonists had their greatest growth – a growth to which our great republic is indebted for the triumphs of the past, the blessings of the present, and the hopes of the future.

A country is known and measured largely by its products. Cotton and corn, horses and cattle, timber and minerals are indeed valuable products; but the greatest possible products of a people or a country are great men and women. Measured by this rule the colonists must have been a great people, for they produced Washington, Franklin, Adams, Jefferson, Hamilton, Greene, Henry, Hancock, Madison, and many others noted in civil and military life. Under these leaders they fought successfully the battles of the Revolutionary War. They did something even greater than that – they founded the great and good government under which we live.

The Call of the West

When the Revolutionary War came to an end, the soldiers returned to their homes and resumed the pursuits of peaceful life. Many of them found their farms in a sad plight. The barns were in decay, the fences gone, and the fields and gardens covered with bushes and briers. They had no money with which to hire help or to buy the things they so much needed. But "where there is a will there is a way." They had the will, and the way sooner or later followed, though it led through much toil and many hardships. Some of them left their old farms and moved to new settlements, where the soil was fresh and more fertile.

Beyond the Allegheny Mountains was a vast unknown

wilderness stretching away toward the sunset. In it were great forests and wide plains, and many rolling rivers and dense canebrakes. The Indians inhabited it, and countless buffaloes browsed on the plains; bears, panthers, and wolves roamed in the forests and canebrakes. Some daring men had gone into these wilds and brought back wonderful reports of the richness of the soil, the beauty of the rivers, and the abundance and variety of the timber, the fish, and the game.

These reports caused many of the settlers to turn their eager eyes and souls to the west. Very soon many families and companies of men and women began to move across the mountains and into the wilds which lay beyond. Some went in the hope of gain, and some in answer to the call of the wild. This love of the wild shows itself, more or less, in all men and boys. There are few lads who do not like to ramble in the woods, swim in the streams that flow through the forests, and play Robinson Crusoe on their lonely islands.

Strange, indeed, it is that anyone should prefer life in the woods, with its exposures and privations, to the comforts of home. Yet there are those to whom the call of the wild is stronger than the love of ease and comfort, or the dread of toil and hunger, or the fear of disease and danger. With a few congenial friends they find delight in hunting wild beasts in the trackless swamps, fishing in wildwood streams, and eating coarse meals in the deep shadows of the forest. Stranger still that this joy in wild life is often greatest when danger is most threatening and the ills most severe. No doubt this love of the wild was implanted in man for a wise purpose. To it is due primarily the extension of man's rule over the earth. In our own country, as in many others of the past, the men who answered the call of the wild were the pioneers of civil life. Without them vast regions, with all their wealth of soil, timber, and mines, would probably have still been unknown, and wild beasts would yet be roaming over fertile tracts where corn and cotton now grow. It may be that the call of the wild was at least a stimulus to the explorations of discoverers like Columbus and Fremont, Livingston, Stanley, and Roosevelt.

The Westward Movement

Accustomed as we are now to good highways, automobiles, railroads, and steamboats, it is hard for one to realize how rough was the way and meager the means of traveling in the days of our forefathers. In moving from the east to the west the pioneers usually went in ox wagons. They carried only small outfits of bedding, clothing, and utensils. Among these "necessary things" were frying pans, axes, and guns. For the sake of company, and for help and protection in time of need, two or more families generally moved together. Often the roads, when there were any, had to be "cleared out" or causewayed. Hampered in this and many other ways the progress was slow. With the close of day camp was pitched near a spring or running branch, if possible. Beds were "fixed" in the wagons for the women and children and pallets made under the trees for the men and boys. As the blackness of night closed about them there came many dismal sounds from the woods – maybe the howl of a wolf, the hoot of an owl, the bark of a fox, or the yell of an Indian.

But with all their scanty means of travel and comfort the trip was to them more enjoyable than onerous. Never having known of the arts and ease of modern life, they did not miss the comforts or conveniences. Just as a citizen of Atlanta enjoys for the first time the sights of Washington, so these denizens of the country were cheered and charmed by the new woodland scenes that constantly opened before them. Indeed, there is nothing in city life which so thrills the heart of man as the wild sense of freedom which the pioneer feels in the wilderness.

People spread over the West from the East by degrees. Going some distance westward they bought or preempted land, built houses, and opened farms. After living on these farms for some time, maybe many years, they or their children moved to places still farther west, and so on, thus gradually encroaching on the hunting ground of the Red man, and converting it into a land of homes, farms, and schools. It may be worth while to note why and how this change went on thus by degrees.

When the land was first cleared the virgin soil, as it was called, was very fertile and produced large crops of everything planted in it. But the crops fed on and consumed the richness of the soil just as a horse feeds on and eats up corn. Much of this rich soil was also washed away by the rains. The method of farming was a wasteful one, because little was done to restore the plant food which the crops took from the soil, and little provision was made to keep the soil from washing away; so that, sooner or later, the fields being pretty well worn out, the owners would "sell out," and move farther west to obtain fresh land.

All the settlers, more or less, had horses, mules, cattle, and hogs, and these were called stock.

In the fresh wild woods, especially during the spring, summer, and fall, there was a quantity of good food for the stock, such as grass, cane, acorns, beechnuts, and pine masts. The woods where this food abounded were called ranges. When new settlers came along they would buy or enter a portion of the land, and therefore, year by year, the ranges became smaller and poorer. To procure better ones, the owners would sell out and move farther west.

In the wild regions where there were but few, if any, settlers, the woods abounded in deer, turkeys, bears, ducks, and other kinds of animals and birds that were good to eat. These were called game, and in the new settlements it formed a large part of the people's food. But, as the number of settlers increased game became scarcer, and by and by, many would seek a locality farther west, where it was more plentiful.

To some the call of the wild was always a stimulus to go west. The desire for adventure and the excitement that attends the discovery of new wonders in Nature's handiwork, appealed to them and in addition to the mere joy of life in the wilds, with its accompanying good health, there was also much profit to be made by securing and selling the hides and furs of such animals as bears, foxes, beavers, otters, and minks.

An Illustration of the Westward Movement

In the cemetery at Tuskegee, Alabama, there is a tombstone bearing this inscription:

In Memory of
Harris Nicholson,
A Revolutionary Soldier;
Who Was Born on the 12th Day of March,
A.D. 1760, and Departed This Life on the
28th Day of June 1841; Aged 81 Yr., 3 Mo., 16 Days

The ancestors of this old soldier came from Scotland, and settled in the Colony of Maryland. Soon after the Revolutionary

War, Harris moved from Maryland to Virginia and thence to Georgia, whether in hopes of gain or in answer to the call of the wild, it is not known. Probably both incentives had something to do with it. He had three sons, all born in Virginia, one of whom was called James. James did not take much to guns and hounds. His activities were due far more to the hope of gain than to the call of the wild. Having a business turn, and being industrious and saving, "he laid up treasures on earth" until he became very well off for a pioneer farmer. He had five sons, all of whom were named after men noted in politics or religion; namely, Matthew, Washington, Monroe, Absalom, and Wesley. From Georgia he moved to Alabama, settling first in Autauga and later in Macon County. This was before the Indians had been driven out of the State. Near the pretty little city of Tuskegee, James Nicholson lived and died. There, by his venerable father, he, his wife, and his son Wesley are buried.

It was in Alabama that Washington, the second son, grew from boyhood to manhood. In business matters and habits he was more or less like his father, but very unlike him in regard to the chase and the wilds. Being a great lover of the woods and all kinds of field sports, he was to be found in the forest or swamp with his gun or his fishing rod when not busy with work on the farm. As he grew older he came to be known as "Uncle Wash," and it is by that name that he is designated in the opening chapter of these chronicles.

During the same period there lived near Tuskegee another well-to-do James, whose surname was Wafer. The Wafers came originally from Ireland, and settled in South Carolina. Now the Scotch James and the Irish James were neighbors and good friends, and this paved the way to friendly relations between Washington and Miss Martha, the younger daughter of the Irish James. Washington came to admire Martha for her genial Irish qualities, and she him for his sturdy Scotch endowments. So, in the natural course of human events, they became man and wife.

This goodly couple, strong in body and clean in morals, were the father and mother of Nick, the hero of this book.

The careers of Matthew and Monroe Nicholson, brothers of Uncle Wash, furnish additional examples of the westward movement. The former, Matthew, early espoused the cause of the "Lone Star State," and after following the fortunes of Sam Houston, joined his friend Walker, the "filibuster," and died in his service in Nicaragua. Monroe served under General Taylor throughout the Mexican War, and subsequently settled in Texas. The children of these two brothers now reside in that great State.

To continue this illustration of the movements to the west we might here run ahead of our story to say that Nick was carried in infancy to Louisiana, where he grew to manhood, was married and became the father of three sons. These, in the course of time, moved still farther west. Two of them now live in Texas, and a short time since the third was driven out of Mexico by the insurgents. Similarly, there are countless other Southern families whose sojournings in the westward movement may be traced from the Potomac to the Rio Grande.

CHAPTER THREE
The Story of a Westward Move

More "Elbow Room"

Although eastern Alabama at that time (1844) was a comparatively new country, Uncle Wash began to look about for a still newer one. Said he, "I want more elbow room." He had heard much of a land called Louisiana lying away beyond the great Mississippi River. He longed to till its fertile soil, browse his stock on its wide and rich ranges, and hunt the wild animals in its forests and canebrakes. He thought of it as "the promised land" and to that far away region he resolved to go. His family at that time consisted of himself, wife, and three children, little Nick being the baby.

Just here we may recall a custom of "large slave owners," that is, men who owned quite a number of Negro slaves. When a son or daughter married, the "old folks" would give him or her a few Negroes. The child generally knew, years in advance, which of the slaves these would be, and the slaves also knew. In kindhearted families, as most of the Dixie families were, there always sprang up a close tie between the child and his or her promised Negroes. Indeed, the servants came to have for their "young massa" or "young missis" a paternal or fraternal affection. In dividing the Negroes among the White children real family ties were seldom if ever severed, unless the change was agreeable to the Negroes themselves.

In accordance with this custom, Uncle Wash had received

from his father and his wife's father, both of whom were then living, the following Negroes: Uncle Nathan and his wife (Aunt Jane), Aunt Kitty and her daughter Mary (the house girl), Claricy (a woman), and Caroline (Nick's nurse).

There were, at that time, two usual routes of travel from Alabama to Louisiana: First, the "overland route" which was traveled in wagons, and led through the State of Mississippi and across the great swamp of the "Father of Waters" and that river itself at Vicksburg, Rodney, or Natchez; second, the "water route" which was more comfortable, by the way of Mobile and New Orleans. Movers having a large number of Negroes and much stock often sent them by the first route and took their families by the second. Uncle Wash took his family and his slaves by the water route.

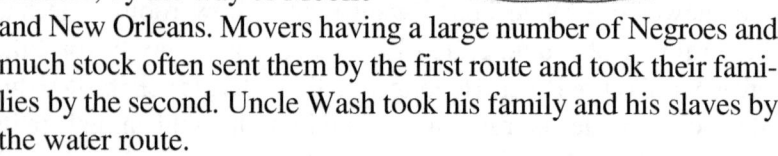

Off For Louisiana

"Good-by! Good-by!" was uttered many times in sorrow and in tears, as Uncle Wash and his party seated themselves in the wagons which were to carry them from Tuskegee to Montgomery; and for some distance a shadow of sadness hovered over them. But it was a bright September morning, and all the landscape was brilliant with sunshine. Here and there the country was threaded with little streams whose rippling waters inspired hope and gladness. These cheering scenes tended to lighten the hearts and brighten the eyes of the movers.

At Montgomery they took a boat, went down the Alabama River to Mobile, and thence across the gulf to New Orleans. For the first time in their lives they were out of sight of land. Aunt Martha amused herself by watching the "servants"; she never called them slaves or Negroes. Uncle Wash also enjoyed seeing them "see things," though he pretended not to notice it. He smiled when Nathan, standing on the bow of the vessel and looking all around to where the sky and sea seemed to come together, said, "It sho' do look like we'se in er kind er low place wi' high lan' all roun' us."

At one time the boat was tossed by a great wave just as Aunt Kitty was crossing the deck. She slipped and fell with such a crash as to jar the boat and startle the passengers. This time Uncle Wash laughed outright, and so did every one present except Aunt Martha, who rushed to the fallen one, helped her up, and assisted her to her couch. After that, no coaxing could induce Aunt Kitty to leave the safest retreat she could find. Aunt Martha visited the servants to see how they were getting along, and finding Aunt Jane packing away some food said, "Jane, what are you doing?"

"Miss Marfy, I'se been frowin' up dreadful, and Nathan he 'lowed I had de sea complaint; so I'se des puttin' up a little vi'tals to eat when us come to de udder side."

They landed at Milneburg, and from there went on "The Pontchartrain Railroad" to the city of New Orleans, a distance of about six miles. This is said to be the second oldest railroad in America. At that time there were three others in the State nearly as old; viz., one from New Orleans to Carrollton, one from Port Hudson to Clinton, and one from Bayou Sara to Woodville, Mississippi. Surely the people living in this section at that time must have been progressive and more or less wealthy.

At one time on the way Uncle Nathan was gazing intently out of a window, just as the train was flying by a field in which the rows were at right angles to the track.

"Nathan," said Aunt Jane, "what is yer starin' at so out'n dat winder?"

"Dem rows," said Nathan, "sho do look like spokes of a big wheel all turnin' roun' a hub way out yonder in de woods."

When the train stopped and the party alighted, Claricy said, "Dat sho' do beat me."

"What yer talkin' 'bout now, nigger?" asked Uncle Nathan.

"Why, God-er-mighty, man," said Claricy, "I didn't mor'n git on dat sof' seat 'fore I had to git out."

New Orleans Then and Now

New Orleans was then a small place in comparison with what it is now. The principal business streets at that time were Royal and Chartres, and the main residence street was Esplanade. The city did not extend much above Canal Street. What is now called Howard Avenue was the boundary of the suburbs, and all beyond that, away up to Carrollton, was woods. The railroad from New Orleans to Carrollton went through these woods, and the roadbed of that old railway is now largely the beautiful St. Charles Avenue. The depot was on the lot now occupied by the public library.

New Orleans was founded by the French in 1718, and in the course of time more and more people came from France to make their homes there. Among these were members of many of the oldest, wealthiest, and most cultured families of Paris. Thus this leading city of Dixie, in the social, industrial, and commercial habits of its citizens, and in the style of its private and public buildings, became the Paris of the new world. After a while the English-speaking people began to settle in the place. They moved in slowly at first, but after about 1845 they poured in at a rapid rate. They settled mostly in, and built up, that part of the city lying above Canal Street. Thus Canal became the central street, and on and across this great broadway played the forces which made New Orleans the charming French-English city that it is. Its population is unique in that it is more or less a cross between the sturdy and thrifty Scotch-English and the artistic and chivalrous French. We may say of them what Macaulay said of the Irish: "They have the qualities which make people interesting rather than prosperous." And this is no bad thing to say about anybody. As a commendation it is better than the reverse, though it may not be so regarded by some in this money-loving age.

However, as stated by Mark Twain, "New Orleans is outfitted with progressive men – thinking, sagacious, long-headed men." In the face of adverse industrial and economic changes wrought by the Civil War, the city has had a steady growth in population and material prosperity. It has met its problems in sanitation, economics, and education bravely and skillfully. The

bank deposits and clearances bear testimony to its financial welfare; and artistic and noble public buildings bespeak its civic pride and elegant discernment. Nowhere are parks more inviting and restful, nor works of art more varied and attractive. Throughout the city are numerous homes, both palatial and humble, that tell their own story of taste and comfort and hospitality. Few cities have more efficient public schools, and fewer still enjoy the advantages and blessings of a great university like Tulane.

In the meantime, New Orleans has not forgotten that:

> We may live without poetry, music and art;
> We may live without conscience, and live without heart;
> We may live without friends; we may live without books;
> But civilized man cannot live without cooks.

The traveling public may be unmindful of the city's great buildings and parks, but of its cuisine never. Nowhere has coffee a more delightful aroma or meat a more savory flavor. No less noted are the New Orleans oysters – renowned alike for their abundance and their quality. The festive board with its viands and good cheer has played an important role in the life of this city of Dixie; and the many bright and generous things which have been said and done there are largely responsible for the reputed "qualities which make the people more interesting than prosperous."

Uncle Wash and his party stopped at the St. Charles, which was said to be "the handsomest hotel, not only in the United States, but in the world." Before going to dinner Aunt Martha said to her husband, "Now, my dear, you must remember not to eat with your knife, nor pick your teeth at the table; and be sure to sip your soup quietly from the side of your spoon."

Of course he had been taught these things at home from childhood, but life in the woods had made him careless about, and almost indifferent to, these "highfalutin' manners." A hint that his manners were not first class nettled him, and he pretended to know exactly what to do without being told by anybody.

"I'll do the best I can," said he rather sullenly, "but I tell you now, it will be precious little soup that I'll get if I have to sip it from the side of a spoon. I call that tomfoolery."

Like most country people they thought when they entered the dining hall that all eyes were centered on them. This put Uncle Wash on his best behavior; so he watched Aunt Martha on the sly, and by following her lead, was proud to think that his conduct had been such as to show those city folks that "he knew a thing or two" himself.

After dinner they stood on the beautiful veranda of the hotel, and looked out over the city. In the street below them people and vehicles of many descriptions moved hither and thither, and beyond lay blocks of massive buildings following each other in endless perspective. The noise of it all rose and fell like the roar of the sea about them. How different was this sound from that of the woods. Here it was as the roar of battle – sharp, harsh, and discordant. In the woods the countless voices of nature produce no discords; the country is never out of tune with itself. "Its music is one vast elemental chord and has been the same for all time."

They spent the afternoon in "seeing the sights." Of course they went to the French Market, and the many interesting and curious things they saw and heard there gave them something to talk about for many a day to come. Among other places and things they saw were the mint, where silver dollars were being coined; the ships, with their tall masts and fine cabins; the bird stores, where many kinds of pretty birds were for sale; and the St. Louis Hotel, with its ballrooms "unequaled in the United States for size and beauty."

Aunt Martha, always thoughtful of the children and servants, took them with her to all these places, not only for their amusement and instruction, but for the pleasure she derived from their droll and witty comments on the things they saw and heard. At the French Market, Uncle Nathan, looking at some tawny foreigners, said, "For de life er me I don't see how dey tells de White folks from de niggers down here." An Italian was vending fruit and speaking loudly and rather musically in a jumble of the English and Italian languages. Nathan gazed at him as if looking at a clown in a circus, and said, "Dat must be sum kin' er corn song he singin'." Aunt Kitty, who could not see very well, ran against a metallic statue of an Indian used in advertising cigars. She hustled around it in a hurry, exclaiming, "I run'd smack into dat gent'-man; I wonder what he standin' out dar like dat fur? Dey sho' do have sum po' White trash down here!"

Never was a trip more thoroughly enjoyed by all, White and Black; and I doubt not that all rejoiced in the thought that they had now added to their list of sights many things that others had not seen.

Up the Red River

The next day a flag was flying from the jack staff of a Red River boat, and also a smaller one from the verge staff astern. This signified that the boat would leave that day. The usual time of departure was 5 o'clock, P.M. As that time drew nearer things became more lively about the boat; quantities of barrels and boxes were rushed across the levee, on to the stage-planks, and aboard the steamer. In the midst of this hurly-burly the passengers made their way to the boat as best they could, many of them carrying one or more huge packages. To our little company, it all looked like a drove of hustling ants almost covered by their big burdens of plunder. Among other things Uncle Wash had a basket of fishing tackle, and a new double-barreled shotgun guaranteed "to shoot buckshot through an inch-plank at a distance of one hundred yards."

Great masses of black smoke rose from the tall chimneys and drifted like clouds over the city.

By and by the throttle valve of the powerful engine was opened, the great driving wheel began to turn, and the vessel glided backward into the deep water. Soon she made a graceful swing, and with her prow pointed up stream, began her journey on the Father of Waters.

By the time the boat was fairly under way the passengers had secured their staterooms, and found comfortable seats on the open promenade deck overlooking the river

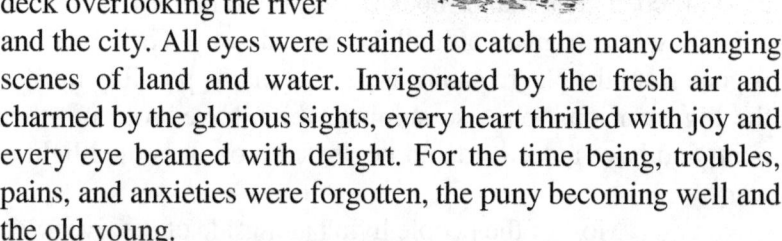

and the city. All eyes were strained to catch the many changing scenes of land and water. Invigorated by the fresh air and charmed by the glorious sights, every heart thrilled with joy and every eye beamed with delight. For the time being, troubles, pains, and anxieties were forgotten, the puny becoming well and the old young.

But there was another scene on the after deck that is worthy of notice. In that quiet place three congenial spirits formed a little coterie of their own. How soon "birds of a feather flock together." Creatures "of a kind" are drawn together by a power as invisible and as certain as the force of gravity. Of no other kind is this more true than of hunters and fishermen. Each of these three was exploiting the merits of his new double-barreled shotgun. Uncle Wash told what his "Mary Ann" was guaranteed to do.

"From what the fellow told me about my 'Nancy Jane,'" said Mr. A., "she's going to kill 'em so high up they'll spoil before they hit the ground."

"That's nothing," said Mr. B., "I am fearing that 'Martha Washington' is going to kill 'm so dead they won't fall."

In 1827 Mrs. Trollope wrote: "The unbroken flatness of the banks of the Mississippi continued unvaried for many miles above New Orleans; but the graceful and luxuriant palmetto, the dark and noble ilex, and the bright orange were everywhere to be seen, and it was many days before we were weary of looking at them."

In the same year Captain Basil Hall wrote: "The district of country which lies adjacent to the Mississippi, in the lower parts of Louisiana, is everywhere thickly peopled by sugar planters, whose showy houses, gay piazzas, trig gardens, and numerous slave villages, all clean and neat, gave an exceedingly thriving air to the river scenery."

"From New Orleans to Baton Rouge," wrote Mark Twain in 1882, "the great sugar plantations border both sides of the river all the way, and stretch their league-wide levels back to the dim forest walls of bearded cypress in the rear. A most homelike and happy-looking region. And now and then you see a pillared and porticoed great manor-house embowered in trees." "But," he continues, "the trigness of it all has passed away. The whitewash is gone from the Negro cabins now; and many, possibly most of the big mansions, once so shining white, have worn out their paint and have a decayed and neglected look. It is the blight of war."

Most of the people living alongside of the river were French. Indeed South Louisiana (all that part lying south of the mouth of Red River) was settled largely by French emigrants from Acadia and France, and most of the present inhabitants of that section are of French descent. These Creoles, as they are called, are kind, polite and industrious, and among them are some of the richest men in the State. By their high ideals and courtly bearing many of them show that the blue blood of the old French aristocracy flows in their veins. They have furnished many of the leaders of Dixie in civil and military life, among whom were Audubon, the naturalist; Gayarré and Fortier, the historians; Beauregard, the general and engineer; and Paul Morphy, possibly the greatest chess player of all times. One of their number, Alexander Mouton, was then (1844) governor of the State. He had before that represented Louisiana in the United States Senate, and while he was residing in Washington the celebrated sculptor Powers carved "The Greek Slave." In selecting a model hand for this famous statue he is said to have chosen that of Mrs. Mouton, who was noted alike for the beauty of her face and the symmetry of her form.

The next morning our boat reached Baton Rouge, one hundred and thirty miles from New Orleans. Here is the first highland – a beautiful bluff country fifty-five feet above sea level, and twelve feet above the highest overflow ever known in the Mississippi Valley. "There was a tropical sun overhead and a tropical swelter in the air," yet it is never so hot or so cold as in places much farther north. In the dark green woods are countless magnolias, whose flowers are seldom surpassed for size, beauty or fragrance. These fertile bluff lands, rising and sinking in graceful curves, well-wooded and well-watered, the home of sunshine, birds and flowers, appear to have been in no way slighted in their making. Baton Rouge was then a sleepy village; now it is a brisk city of 23,000 souls, the capital of the State, and the site of the Louisiana State University.

Twenty miles above Baton Rouge is Port Hudson, a place of historic interest and modern unimportance. Just as the alluvial lands on the east bank give way to the bluffs at Baton Rouge, so here at Port Hudson the bluffs give place to the hills. These high hills, overlooking the river, were the scenes of some severe conflicts in the Civil War. One of these was the night battle between Farragut's fleet and the Confederate land batteries, April 14, 1863.[1]

---

1. Nick was there on the memorable night of April 14th, but, being sergeant of the guard, was in a place of comparative safety – the hot balls and lighted bombs passed mostly over his head. While the superb pyrotechnic display was in operation, he wrote the following parody on an old hymn:

> When I can see a blazing bomb,
> Come whizzing through the sky,
> I bid farewell to every fear,
> As round a stump I fly.

This landscape was the first to remind Aunt Martha of the hills about her old Georgia home. With Nick in her arms, a tear stole down her cheek as the scene awakened in her memories of loved ones far away. How fortunate she did not then know that that baby boy, eighteen years thereafter, would be on that very spot to take part in one of the most terrific struggles of modern times.[2]

Fifty miles above Port Hudson the Red River pours its its reddish water into the Mississippi, and this tributary, forty miles above its mouth, receives the dark blue waters of the Ouachita. These two rivers, Red and Ouachita, recede from one another northward and cross the north boundary of the State more than a hundred miles apart. That part of Louisiana lying between these two rivers is what we call "North Central Louisiana." It comprises about one-fifth of the State, is a high upland region, and is well timbered; and through it flow numberless branches and creeks of clear sweet water. Many of these streams rise in Claiborne Parish, which is adjacent to Arkansas and on the dividing ridge between the two bordering rivers.

The most fertile lands in the State are the valleys of its great rivers, and it may seem queer that the settlers (English) from the older States did not secure places in these richer districts. That they did not do so, as a rule, is due to two causes: (1) they naturally sought a country more or less like that from which they came, and this they found in North-Central Louisiana, with its hills and valleys, clear running streams, and springs or wells of pure water; (2) they feared the river lands would not be

---

2. At Jackson, La., which is about twelve miles from Port Hudson, was Centenary College, a splendid and noted institution before the Civil War. It is now located in Shreveport.

healthful. While the highlands were not as fertile as the lowlands, they had a rich virgin soil and many beautiful and productive upland valleys. Here was the promise of health, pleasure, and at least a plenty of products.

Uncle Wash's objective point was some place in Claiborne Parish, and his route lay up the Red River to Shreveport, and thence sixty miles east by wagons into the very heart of "the promised land." Landing at Shreveport, which was then a small town, he pitched camp on the spot (then in the woods) where the Majestic Theater now stands.

From the very first, Shreveport has had all the accessories necessary to a steady and healthy growth. It lies at the head of navigation on the Red River, is the center of a most fertile region, was a frontier supply point for eastern Texas (then Mexico), and later became the beneficiary of immense oil beds and the largest gas field in America. Fortunately its citizens have had the patriotism and the good business judgment to make the best use of their superb opportunities. From a small pioneer village of two or three stores, as Nick first saw the place, it has expanded into a magnificent city of 35,000 population, having ninety-five industries and seventy-five wholesale houses, forty-two miles of paved streets, eleven million dollars of bank deposits and eleven lines of railroads, together with public buildings, churches, and schoolhouses unsurpassed in architecture and equipments.

Uncle Wash, having secured the necessary teams and wagons, crossed the Red River and started east on the "home stretch" of the long journey. He soon discovered that the road in the swamp was unlike any he had seen in the older States. As the wagon and oxen sank deep into the soft red mud, Uncle Nathan remarked, "Dis road don't 'pear to have no bottom." The swamp of the Red River is about ten miles wide, and was then almost impassable on account of the many bogs and unbridged sloughs. These places, according to a saying of the settlers, "would bog the shadow of a buzzard." But the instant the situation became strenuous, Uncle Wash became alert and settled into the grim reserve that characterizes the man who takes any enterprise seriously, be it work or play.

The whole day was occupied in crossing the swamp. Just as the sun was setting, the travelers, wet, tired, muddy and hungry, reached the piny uplands which form the eastern boundary of the great valley. Here they went into camp, and began at once to "clean up" and "dry up" – ridding the stock and wagon of mud and themselves of wet and muddy clothes. This "task of ablution and abstersion" being performed, and a frugal but hearty meal eaten, Uncle Wash stretched himself out on his improvised bed of cane tops and blankets.

"My dear," said Aunt Martha, "you have certainly earned a night's repose. Your day's work has been hard and steady, and few could have managed it all so well."

"Martha," he answered, "often the only, and always the surest, way of doing a thing is by plugging away at it. That's my principle in life. Keep at it. In work, as in hunting, that's the way to win. True, the way is hard, but overcoming difficulties is the glorious part of it. If success comes easy, we care but little for it;

if it comes hard, we never forget the ways and means. I believe the real value of a thing to anyone is to be measured by the labor and skill it cost that one to get it."

Early the next morning the party moved on into the dense woods. What there was of road, though narrow and rough, was at least firm, a quality of the soil that is always appreciated by the traveler, especially just after crossing a "bottomless swamp." Thirty miles from Shreveport they crossed the Bayou Dorchete, which in season is navigable up to Minden. Beyond this stream the surface of the land was more elevated and undulating, having an average altitude of 200 feet above sea level and countless hills and valleys running in every direction.

Far in the interior of North-Central Louisiana is a pretty little stream, called Parker's Creek. On the banks of this perennially flowing streamlet a pioneer had made a settlement consisting of a few cabins and a field of twenty acres. Desiring to move farther west so as to get "more elbow room," he "sold out" to Uncle Wash, who took immediate possession. With the cabins renovated and enlarged and more land opened, Uncle Wash stayed here two years and then moved to a new and better place, as described in the opening chapter of this book.

CHAPTER FOUR
The Story of a Typical Neighborhood

Uncle Wash Moves From Cane Ridge

Early in the year 1853 Uncle Wash moved to a place some fifteen miles west of Cane Ridge. His main object was to get in a neighborhood which gave promise of maintaining a good school. Nick, now in his ninth year, went with Aunt Kitty in the ox wagon, of which Uncle Nathan was the driver. The rest of the party, having faster teams, went on ahead. Nick had Step, the fice, with him.

The boy was wild with joy, thrilled with visions of coming scenes and events. Nothing along the way escaped his notice. Here and there were branches whose clear water flowed over pretty pebbles with a sweet murmur. A hornet's nest, shaped like a watermelon, hung from the limb of an oak, and away up in the top of a tall pine an eagle's nest looked grand and lonely. In the bark of many beech trees were long scratches made by bears in climbing for beechnuts. Now and then Aunt Kitty gave Nick a ginger-cake smeared with jam. They stopped to get some water at the Sulphur Springs, and Aunt Kitty remembered this as the place where old Bee, the buggy mule, once got into a yellow jacket's nest.

Nick often got out of the wagon and played with Step along the road. Now and then a rabbit sprang out of its hiding place and Step chased it off into the woods. At one time Step set up a furious barking in the bushes near the road, and all hands went to see what it was about. Step had found an enemy and looked as if he was about to charge it, but he was very careful to keep at a safe distance from the object of his wrath. It was a monster rattlesnake, as large around as a man's arm, wound into a great coil, and making a hideous noise with its rattles as if warning everybody to keep away. Uncle Nathan killed it with a stick.

There were eighteen rattles on the end of its tail, which showed, according to the settler's rule, that it was eighteen years old.

Here and there new settlements were to be seen. People were then moving into North-Central Louisiana at a rapid rate. They came mostly from Alabama and Georgia, but there were many from all the Southern States, and a few from the North. These new settlers were active, pushing people, as settlers usually are. That they have a purpose to better their condition, and the industry necessary to undertake it, is shown by their very presence in the vanguard of civilization.

The long stillness of the woods was being broken by the hum of industry; the merry song of the hammer and the sweet rasp of the saw, mingled with the cheering crow of the rooster and the stirring "gee" and "haw" of the plowman. The smoke from burning logs and brush hovered over the "new-grounds," and the air was redolent with the odor of fresh burnt woods. The ax and the maul, the hoe and the plow, were invading the dominion of bears and panthers, wolves and catamounts. Indeed, these wild animals had almost disappeared; only a few straggling ones could be seen now and then.

Among other things that had disappeared were wild pigeons. While Uncle Wash was living at Cane Ridge they came annually, sometimes appearing in droves of thousands. Nick often saw flocks of them so large as to darken the heavens like great black clouds. They roosted at night on bushes, and kept up such a clamor that they could be heard a mile or more. Near the road was a grove of very crooked pine trees. Pointing to it Uncle Nathan said, "Dat was once a pigin roos'; de pigins bent 'em up dat way roos'in on 'em when dey was pine bushes."

In those days there were many violent storms in that section, the wrecks of which are still to be seen in many places. Early in the afternoon Nathan, looking up into the skies, said: "I do b'leve we's gwine to have a storm." Sure enough, after a while, dark clouds began to roll over their heads; then came flashes of lightning and distant peals of thunder. Even the oxen seemed to know that a storm was coming, for they struck a quicker gait, as if wishing to get out of the tall timber as soon as they could.

The storm was just bursting upon them as they reached the new settlement of Mr. McClendon. He saw the wagon coming, and running to it as fast as he could he told Nathan to drive the team into an open place just ahead, grasped Nick with one hand and Aunt Kitty with the other, and ran to a stout log cabin that was occupied by his family. His larger log residence was not then finished. Everybody was soon huddled in the cabin. As the storm grew in uproar and vehemence, all became more frightened. It is queer that people who are ordinarily fearless will cower and tremble in the presence of a storm. In their eagerness to get into the safest place possible the men made an opening in the floor by removing two puncheons, and through this opening all hands, White and Black, went under the house. The storm raged and roared. It was hard to tell which was the louder, the howl of the winds or the roar of the thunder.

After a while the storm passed away, leaving behind it a wide area of blown-down trees. Had the cabin been in the main path, it would have been swept away. Fortunately no one was hurt, but the place was almost hemmed in by fallen timber. Mr. McClendon at once sent a runner to inform Uncle Wash that "the

folks, team, and wagon were all right. Such was the kindness with which the settlers treated one another, especially in time of trouble or sickness.

After the storm, for some distance the wagon made slow progress, because Uncle Nathan often had to stop to clear the road of logs and tree-tops. Late in the afternoon they passed the home of Mr. Tippit, and there Nick saw two things he never saw before: brick chimneys and glass windows.

Progressive Development

They reached their new home after dark. Uncle Wash had been there the year before and built several of the necessary houses. They were not finished except as to walls, roofs, and floors. It was too late to put up beds; so all slept on mattresses laid on the floors, and being tired, they slept soundly. Uncle Wash woke them early the next morning, for he knew there was much to be done.

The residence was an eight-room house, having brick chimneys and glass windows, a wide hall, and a wide gallery in front. The other buildings and appurtenances, – kitchen, dairy, pantry, smokehouse, Negro quarters, shops, ginhouse, cotton press, garden, barns, horse lot, stalls, cow pen, and fields – were located according to a systematic plan. The three main objects of this orderly arrangement were convenience, cleanliness, and attractiveness. The Negro quarters consisted of two long rows of comfortable cabins separated by a "street" two hundred and fifty feet wide. The "big house" was at one end of this street and the shops at the other.

The number of Negroes had very much increased. Some of the new ones had been bought, but the most of them came from the estate of Uncle Wash's father. Among these latter was old Uncle Jack, the first Negro ever owned by Nick's grandfather.

"Martha," said Uncle Wash to his wife at the breakfast table, "I know the houses are not finished, but they have good roofs and will do to live in for a while. The main work to be done is clearing the land and raising a crop. So I'm going to put all hands to doing this work."

"Now, dear," replied Aunt Martha, "that is all right if you will let me have Uncle Jack. With him, Kittie, Caroline, Mary and the boys (her sons Mat, Nick, and Tate), I can begin to put things in order about the house, dairy, kitchen, and smokehouse."

"That can be done for the present," said Uncle Wash, "but I will soon need the boys to work with the 'trash gang.'"

Anyone, male or female, who did full work on the farm was called a "hand." But there was always certain light work that the children could do, and the boys and girls so assigned formed what was called the "trash gang."

So Aunt Martha began work indoors with the "house gang," and Uncle Wash outdoors with the hands and the "trash gang."

Uncle Wash believed in making his sons work. At every stage of their growth, when they were not in school, tasks were assigned them regularly in the fields and shops. His chief object was to school them in useful ways and habits. In common with thousands he thought that most of the best and greatest men in this world have toiled at the workbench and plow.

Few people know how much hard work it takes to change a heavy-timbered tract of land into a complete field. The way Uncle Wash had it done was, briefly, as follows:

    1. Deaden all the large timber with axes.

    2. Cut the logs into ten-foot pieces, and roll the pieces

into "log heaps."

3. Cut down all the bushes and saplings, trim up the larger ones, and pile the poles and brush into "brush-heaps."

4. Burn the log-heaps and brush-heaps as soon as possible

5. Cut rail timber, split it into rails, and build a worm fence around the field. Wire fences were not then in existence.

6. Plow the ground thoroughly, using "colters" at the first plowing to cut the roots.

Not many landscapes are more unsightly than a "new-ground" just after its first plowing. In the midst of stumps and deadened trees, and tangles of roots and briers, clods and fragments of upturned turf bestrew the earth not unlike molten rocks in a desert plain. It is at best a discouraging prospect.

One day as they were looking over the rough and ragged scene, Aunt Martha said to Uncle Wash, "After all that has been done, how much more hard work it will take to put this in a tillable state. It is enough to dishearten one. I don't see how you can be so cheerful about it."

"Martha," answered he, "I have not much education, but I do know that everything in this world that's worth while comes by hard work. If we keep plugging away at it, success will come after a while. In the meantime, it looks like nature comes in to help us. We will be helped by the winds in felling these trees, by decay in destroying these roots and stumps, and by the sun and rain in pulverizing these clods."

Uncle Wash often illustrated a point with a story. So now he said, "I think there is a fine moral in the old story about Uncle Zeke. Having been asked if his prayers were ever answered, he replied, 'It's owin to de natur of de pertition. You see it's like dis: when I prays to de Lawd to send me one of de boss's fat chickens, de chicken don't come; but when I prays to de Lawd to send me atter de chicken, de chicken is sho to git dar fo' day.'

"That is," said Uncle Wash, "the Lord helps those who do most of the work themselves."

A mile west of Uncle Wash's new place was the beginning of a little village, called Forest Grove. It began with a schoolhouse and a store, the post office being located in the latter. In a few years it became the center of a prosperous neighborhood, and in the meantime a large church, and wood and blacksmith shops were added.

The land in this section was more or less level, just hilly and rolling enough to afford good drainage. Many clear running branches flowed through it, and these, coming together, formed beautiful creeks. The land was easily tilled, and on it a variety of crops could be grown. In a few years many well-to-do farmers settled in the community. They raised cotton chiefly, but also enough corn, oats, potatoes, and meat for home use. They were kind and polite to guests and strangers. No one passing through the country, whether rich or poor, was charged anything for a night's entertainment.

To show how little the men and boys knew or cared for fashion, a funny incident may be related here. When Uncle Wash lived at Cane Ridge he and Dr. Kidd had a little store, and on severing the partnership each took half of the goods. Uncle Wash thus came to have three silk hats.

Failing to sell these "two-story" hats, and seeing that no one desired them, he said to his wife, "Martha, the boys need new Sunday hats, and it seems to me that we can supply them, and at the same time avoid expense, by giving them the three silk hats."

Now Martha, having a great deal of Irish humor as well as Irish blood, at once saw how absurd and yet how funny it would be. So, hiding a smile, she said, "All right, my dear, if you desire it."

Nick was about eleven years old, but there was no trouble in fitting him, as his head was quite large for his age. Paper had to be put in the other two hats to make them small enough.

The next Sunday the boys arrayed themselves in homespun suits, brogan shoes, and "two-story" silk hats. Thus attired they went to church, Mat riding one mule and Tate riding behind Nick on another. Arriving at the church, they dismounted, hitched the mules to the trees, and walked abreast toward the building. They squared their shoulders and stepped proudly when they saw that they were the "observed of all observers." The reader must not infer that Nick was a typical boy of Dixie on that occasion, for it is probable that no other boys of the land were ever rigged out in that way, before or since.

Every farmer had Negroes, more or less. As a rule, they were well cared for, partly because they were valuable property, but mostly on account of the personal regard the Whites had for them. In the case of old family servants this regard amounted to real love on the part of both the Whites and the Blacks. In this community there were exacting but no cruel masters. A place was reserved for the Negroes in the church, and the two races thus worshipped together every Sunday. The writer never saw an exception to this statement by Henry W. Grady: "The one character utterly condemned and ostracised was the man who was mean to his slaves. For the cruel master, there was no toleration."

Year by year the neighborhood improved in every way. The country was becoming pretty thickly settled by civil and industrious people. Following them came better roads and bridges, brickyards and lumber mills, improved stock and vehicles, finer houses and better churches, better schoolhouses and schools, and many comforts unknown in pioneer life.

Every man went to church on Sunday, wearing his best clothes, driving his best team, and putting on his best airs. At the church the mules and horses were hitched to the trees, the women went at once into the building, and the men gathered in front of it, talked of the crops, related personal "stunts," cracked jokes, and chewed tobacco. These performances were presently disturbed by the singing within of some old hymn, as:

> When I can read my title clear
> To mansions in the skies,
> I'll bid farewell to every fear
> And wipe my weeping eyes.

    This was the signal for all to come in, and in they went, hats off, heads up, and eyes to the front. Each looked as if he felt that he was the center of observation.
    The sermons were usually of an hour's length, and on "big occasions" two hours. They were fluent, earnest, and thoughtful. Now and then the climaxes (oral) rose to such heights as to disturb the naps of the old folks.
    After the services, all assembled on the lawn in front of the church and there was a regular epidemic of handshaking, "howdying," and chatting. It seemed as if everybody was trying to get everybody else to "go home with them to dinner." All

strangers and visitors were specially looked after, and if any failed to be well cared for it was his own fault.

"Ben," said John as they rode off together, "why are people so talkative just after coming out of church?"

"It seems to me," said Ben, "that talk just naturally flows out of some people like water out of a spring, and when they have to be silent for a bit, as in a church, it dams up their stream of talk, and the supply thus accumulates until their reservoirs are chock-full. When the bars to speech are removed the flood gates are opened and the pent-up talk pours forth like compressed steam from a mud-valve."

"And the worst of it is," replied John, "no matter what they begin to talk about they always end with talking about themselves."

The Forest Grove School

The school at Forest Grove kept pace with the rapid march of progress everywhere to be seen. In comparison with the Cane Ridge school there were now better books, finer equipments, and fitter teachers. Chief among these books were Davies' arithmetics, Smith's grammar, Mitchell's geographies, McGuffey's readers, and Webster's speller. The switch was still used, but not so much as in the Cane Ridge school. Under the old regime the master went at it as if it were a manly and heroic feat; now the teacher prefaced his floggings by the declaration: "I do this from a sense of duty, and I assure you it does not hurt you one whit more than it does me."

"So we boys and girls," said Mark, "were bound to admit that it was mighty good in him to take such an interest in us, yet we could have wished him less ready to sacrifice himself." The new plan of ruling pupils by "moral suasion" was much spoken of and strongly advocated by persons of "progressive educational ideas." An old-time teacher speaking of it said: "There are cases it will not reach, but you put the rod to them and they will hustle like a terrapin with a coal of fire on his back."

There were no public schools then as we have them now. The patrons, and not the State, employed the teachers and paid them for their services. The tuition fees were $2, $3, and $4 per month, according as the pupil was in a lower or higher class. The State paid the school a small sum, and each patron's pro rata share of this "public money" was deducted from his tuition bill.

The school "took in" at 8 o'clock A.M., and "turned out" at 5 o'clock P.M. In the morning about 10 and in the afternoon about 3:30 there was a short recess. From 12 to 1:30 was "dinner time" and "play time." The playground of the boys was in front of the schoolhouse and that of the girls was in the rear of it. The games played by the boys were town ball, bull pen, roly hole, mumble the peg, marbles, hats, broad and high jumps, three jumps, and "half hammon." Another favorite game was "deer." The boy who could run fastest and longest usually played deer, and all the others were the dogs. The dogs would pursue the deer through the near-by fields and woods, and the chase often lasted during the entire play time.

Up to that time few countries ever sent a greater proportion of their sons to college than did the South. The favorite colleges were Yale, Princeton, and the University of Virginia, though many excellent ones nearer home were liberally patronized. Many of these bright young graduates began life as teachers, expecting later on to take up the study and practice of law, medicine, or engineering. Three of these, Griggs, Simmons, and Boring, were the successive principals of the Forest Grove school, and they were men of ability and culture.

With them the chief end of education was culture, and the basis of all culture was good spelling, reading, and writing. Every student, however high his studies or standing, had to recite once a day in the "big spelling class." The written tests in any subject were "deficient" unless the spelling and writing were good. This is illustrated in the following incident:

Nick and two other lads, Toab and Charlie, were studying elementary algebra. At a certain recitation Toab was sent to the board to solve a problem about dividing an estate between a widow, two sons, and three daughters. According to the requirements he wrote the solution in full, with much regard for form, clearness, spelling, and punctuation. But with all his care he made the mistake of writing "wider" for widow.

"Toab," said the teacher, "I am surprised to see that you do not know how to spell 'widow.'"

Toab at once erased "wider," and with an air which seemed to say, "Of course I know better than that," wrote "widor."

"Charles," said the teacher, "go to the board and show Toab how to spell 'widow.'"

Charles was a vain fellow, and thinking he had a sure thing of it, strutted up to the board, erased "widor" and wrote "widder."

"Nick, go and show those ignorant boys how to spell 'widow,'" ordered the teacher.

Now Nick thought his time of triumph had come, because he could not conceive of more than one other way in which the thing could be done. So he stepped boldly forward, erased "widder" and wrote "widdor."

It is safe to say that, after that impressive schooling, those boys never forgot how to spell that highly respected word.

The funniest stories are those of incidents which actually occurred, like the above and the following one, though they are never so funny in the telling as in the doing of the thing itself.

One of the little fellows was given the word "squirrel" to spell. He hesitated, because he did not know how to make a start, much less how to proceed after he had started. Being pressed by the teacher, and feeling that he just had to do it some way or another, he made a pass at it by exclaiming, "sque-didle-dy."

Every Friday afternoon the students, large and small, had to "speak." Nowadays it is called reciting. Occasionally it was- "public Friday," at which times the parents and the public were invited to attend. On these public occasions the boys and girls wore their Sunday clothes, and were washed and dressed beyond a state of naturalness and comfort.

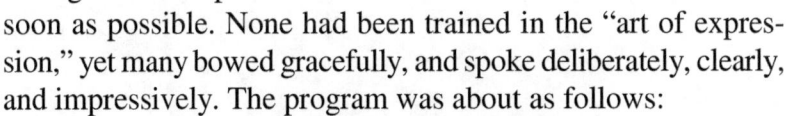

There were reserved seats for the guests. The master called out the speakers, one at a time, beginning with the smallest.

Each speech began and ended with a "bow" – often a quick nod or jerk of the head, as if the speaker wished to get through with the performance as soon as possible. None had been trained in the "art of expression," yet many bowed gracefully, and spoke deliberately, clearly, and impressively. The program was about as follows:

    1. A boy. "I like to see the growing grass,
         Before the farmer mows it,
         I like to see the pacing horse
         'Cause when he goes he goes it."
    2. A girl. "I had a little bunty hen,
         Which mama gave to me,
         Every day she laid' two eggs,
         And Sunday she laid three."
    9. A boy. "The boy stood on the burning deck,
         Whence all but him had fled," and so on.
    10. A girl. "I met a little cottage girl,
         She was eight years old, she said," etc.
    19. A boy. "On Linden when the sun was low,
         All bloodless lay the untrod'n snow."
    20. A girl. "Stay, jailer, stay, and hear my woe," etc.
    49. A boy. "They tell us that we are weak," etc.
    50. A girl. "There was a sound of revelry by night," etc.
    Some v

Little Charlie once began and ended as follows:

        "I like to see a little dog,
        And pat him on the – Oh! – Oh! –"

Thus breaking down, he stammered, "Oh! Mr. Boring, everybody is looking right straight at me."

CHAPTER FIVE
The Story of a Typical Section
☆ ☆ ☆ ☆

Typical of Dixie

As before stated, North-Central Louisiana was settled by English-speaking people – those whose forefathers came from England, Ireland, or Scotland. Few new countries were ever blessed with a better class of citizens. They came from all parts of the South, attracted by the salubrity of the region, the fertility of the soil, and the abundance of pure water, timber, and game. Each of the older States of Dixie was represented there by hundreds of its best men and women. Probably no other section of the South was so typical of Dixie as a whole. There the Virginian, the South Carolinian, the Kentuckian, and the Georgian came together, bringing and blending their ideals, manners, and customs. It was Dixie in a nutshell.

Many towns and cities have crooked streets, owing to their having been built along winding roads or streams. This was not the case with Homer, the county seat of Claiborne Parish. It was located "at the center of the parish." Fortunately the site thus determined (seven miles west of Forest Grove) was a beautiful one, and in the woods. There were no roads, streams, or buildings to interfere with an ideal plan, and the citizens had the good sense to lay off the town in square "blocks." Hence all the streets are straight and cross one another at right angles. The same good taste and judgment were exercised in building the residences and gardens, so that Homer is now, and always has been, one of the prettiest and cleanest inland towns in the South. The courthouse, a two-story building surrounded by an imposing peristyle of massive columns, stands alone on the central square, and facing it on all sides are stores and offices, as in most Southern county seats.

Two Good Signs

Two of the best signs of an alert and progressive people are good roads and good schools. While these, in that section, were in many ways deficient, they were pretty good for a new country. The roads were worked regularly by the people at large, White and Black, under the direction of an overseer appointed by the Police Jury. The streams were well bridged, and the roads through the swamps and low places causewayed. In thinly settled districts the school-houses were often crude and the schools poorly attended; but in the more prosperous neighborhoods the schools were similar to that of Forest Grove.

That some of the schools were of high order is shown by the fact that many of the teachers were graduates of the best colleges of the country. Two of these principals were Edwin Fay, a graduate of Harvard University, who subsequently became the State Superintendent of education, and David F. Boyd, a graduate of the University of Virginia, and afterwards President of the State University.

This promising state of affairs was the outgrowth of a condition and a force which always make for good: (1) the people at large were sturdy and sensible; (2) there were among them many well educated and public-spirited men and women. That some of them were tasty, if not classic, is shown by the names they gave the towns and villages; such as Homer, Athens, Sparta, Lisbon, Minden, Vienna, Tulip, Trenton, Vernon, and Arcadia.

The Gee Place

Twelve miles east of Homer is an old place which has a history of more than local interest on account of its connection with certain noted men and events. This, known as the "Gee Place," has been the scene of many a gay party; and many a traveler, rich and poor, has found a hearty welcome within its walls.

It was settled by Major James Dyer in 1822. He was an old soldier of the war of 1812, and was with General Jackson in the battle of New Orleans. Claiborne Parish was created at his suggestion and largely by his untiring efforts, and he was its first representative in the State legislature. On account of his witty, wise, and terse sayings, he was known as the Benjamin Franklin of the parish. He came from Missouri to Louisiana.

The most noted brigand that ever figured in the land of Dixie was John Murel, and he had much to do, in an indirect way, with making the Gee Place an ideal old Southern home. His home was in Tennessee, but he was the leader of a large band of robbers who stole and sold Negroes, horses, and cattle all up and down the Mississippi Valley. There were gangs of these robbers at different places – in the towns and woods and on the islands in the rivers – and these gangs helped one another in disposing of the plunder.

Murel was a dashing, fine-looking fellow, fairly well educated, and a good speaker. He knew much about the Bible, and when it suited his wicked purposes he pretended to be a preacher. Frequently he preached to assemblies, large and small, and while the people were enjoying his "fine sermons" on good morals and high ideals his men crept up out of the woods and stole their horses.

S. P. Gee was born and reared in Tennessee. He was a bright and well educated man, and began life as a teacher. While yet a young man he moved to Mississippi, and settled near Rocky Springs, a few miles east of Vicksburg. There he met the beautiful Miss Brock, a daughter of one of Mississippi's wealthy planters. Each was attracted by the good qualities of the other, and they became man and wife.

Many good men desired to bring Murel to trial and break up his band of robbers. But they failed to do so, probably on account of the lack of any definite proof as to Murel's guilt, and also because Murel had many friends who would probably have resented his prosecution. Now Mr. Gee had a brave young friend named Stewart, to whom he said, "Stewart, it is not always the things that can be demonstrated of which we are the most sure. I am confident that Murel is a very bad and dangerous man, and if you will get the proofs of it I will prosecute him."

"All right," said Stewart, "I'll do the best I can," and straightway started on his hazardous undertaking. After many unsuccessful attempts, and believing that "the end justified the means" he joined Murel's clan, took the oath, and was given their secret passwords and grips. He then visited several of their camps and learned all all about them.

He brought back such reports of the large number of men in the service of Murel that Mr. Gee laid the matter before the governor of the State, and asked him for the help of the State militia in arresting the outlaws. So Murel was arrested, tried, convicted, and sentenced to the penitentiary. But Gee and Stewart had to leave the State to avoid being killed by some of Murel's men. Mr. Gee sold his property and took his wife to some city in the North. After living there a year he went into the wilds of North Louisiana and bought the Dyer place in 1836. One of Murel's men followed him even to this secluded spot, and would have killed him had it not been for the brave and timely help of one of Mr. Gee's Negro men.

Mr. Gee became one of the wealthiest men in North-Central Louisiana. He built a beautiful home, and surrounded it with pretty gardens, flowers, and walks. His large farm was a model in all that goes to make a farm attractive and productive. The roads through it reminded one of paved streets, and even along the fences and branches there were no weeds or bushes. The spacious barns seemed bursting with corn and fodder, and the horses, cows, and hogs looked as if they felt that way. There was everywhere a seeming rivalry between cleanliness and abundance. Here the traveler found rest and the hungry food, and that "without money and without price."

Mr. Gee died in 1863, and after his death Mrs. Gee told Mr. Hilley, her son-in-law, the following story, making him promise not to repeat it to anyone during her lifetime. The story is in relation to two of Mr. Gee's friends, Major McEnery and Dr. Egan, with whom the reader should have some acquaintance in order to appreciate it.

Major McEnery was a Virginian, a ripe scholar, and an able lawyer. He served in the war of 1812, being the major of a regiment. Subsequently he moved to Louisiana, and settled in Monroe, where he practiced his profession. He was the father of John and Samuel McEnery, both of whom became governors of the State.

Dr. Bartholomew Egan was born in Ireland and educated at Trinity College, Dublin. He was learned in the classics and also in the science and art of medicine. He was brought to this country by Thomas Jefferson to be a professor in the University of Virginia. Later on, he began the practice of medicine, and became the surgeon of the regiment of which McEnery was the major. Some time after the war he moved to North-Central Louisiana, where he lived and died. He was the father of Hon. W. B. Egan, one of the supreme judges of the State, and also of Dr. J. C. Egan, a noted physician of Shreveport.

One cold winter afternoon, away back in the forties, according to Mrs. Gee's story, she, Dr. Egan, and Mr. Gee, were seated by a warm fire in her parlor. There was a "hello" at the front gate, and Mr. Gee, on going out, was rejoiced to see his old friend Major McEnery. As they walked toward the house Mr. Gee casually stated that Dr. Egan had also stopped to spend the night.

The major, halting, said, "Then, you must excuse me; I shall go on to the next place."

"You will do nothing of the kind," said Mr. Gee. "I did

not know of any difference between you and the doctor. If there is any, I can put you in separate rooms."

"No," said the major, "I would not put you to that trouble. I will go in the room where Dr. Egan is, if you and Mrs. Gee will not be offended by my ignoring him altogether."

In the meantime Dr. Egan, looking through the window, saw Mr. Gee and the major enter the front gate, and at once said to Mrs. Gee, "If Major McEnery comes into this room, you and Mr. Gee must permit me to ignore him entirely."

Mr. Gee went alone into the room, had a short conference with his wife and the doctor, and returning to the major said, "It is all right, major; come in."

Seated around a cheerful fire the party talked, told stories, and laughed; but neither the doctor, nor the major made any reply (and seemingly paid no attention) to anything the other said. This conduct continued at the table, during the evening, and the next morning until the visitors left.

Major McEnery was the last to leave; taking his host by the hand, he said, "I owe you and Mrs. Gee an apology, and I ask you to receive my statement in confidence. Dr. Egan and I were

friends in Virginia, and served in the same regiment. We had a quarrel; it led to a duel between us; there was one exchange of shots; each of us called for another; our seconds said that was enough; we separated without being restored to friendship, and so the matter has stood ever since."

Soon after Mrs. Gee's death Mr. Hilley, who now resides in Shreveport, told Nick the story of the Gee Place. Many, many years after that, Samuel McEnery became governor of the State. One day Nick went into the governor's office, and finding him alone, related to him the story of the singular meeting of his father and Dr. Egan.

The governor listened intently to Nick until he finished, and then said, "Nick, every word of that is true, but I did not think anyone knew anything about it except the older members of the two families. Soon after Dr. Egan and my father died their sons came together and agreed not to prolong the feud of their fathers. So the matter was dropped and forgotten, and there are now no closer or warmer friends in the State than the sons of those two good men."

A Peaceful and Prosperous Land

Eight public roads started from Homer and led in different directions, not unlike spokes diverging from the hub of a wheel. Along these thoroughfares, for miles and miles, were beautiful homes and prosperous farms, many of them resembling and rivaling the Gee Place in appearance and magnitude, resources and hospitality. The residences, standing in the center of large grounds, nestled in swelling masses of semi-tropical plants and exotics of many a hue. Everywhere were the signs of an active, tasty, intelligent, and practical population.

The owners of these homes were not generally men of high academic culture, but with a "grammar-school education" they had that culture which comes from handling important affairs, reading current events of Parish, State, and Nation, associating with civil and well-to-do people, and aiming always to play the rôle of "the gentleman" in all their dealings with their neighbors and slaves, and especially with strangers. Of course there were exceptions. Here, as elsewhere, were shiftless men and women, rowdies and blackguards. But, as a rule, the men who directed public affairs and molded public sentiment were upright, intelligent and forceful. Nor were such men confined to any particular walk of life. Men of brains and character were to be found among the lawyers and doctors, ministers and farmers, merchants, educators and editors. A scholar who has read much and traveled more, and who knew that section of the State intimately as it was before the Civil War, recently said, "On the whole, I could have selected an abler body of men from North Louisiana in 1860 than I have ever seen assembled in the capital of any State, North or South."

But the thrifty air of that once prosperous region has disappeared. The town (Homer) has improved, but the surrounding country has deteriorated in many ways. All rejoice in the freedom of the Negro, yet it is a lamentable fact that a number of homes, improvements, and good old customs were swept away when slavery was abolished.

Religion and Churches

When the complete history of the development of the country is written, no part of it will shine with greater splendor and none will furnish more examples of self-sacrificing devotion to duty than the work wrought by the Christian ministers. In sunshine and in showers, often in hunger and in tattered clothes, traveling where there were no roads, and sleeping where there were no beds, they toiled for the spread of the gospel and the betterment of their fellow-creatures. With busybodies of this character northern Louisiana was blessed in every stage of its development.

Churches sprang up in all the towns and villages and at some of the most frequented crossroads. Many of these houses of worship had their origin in brush arbors and crude log cabins, but, with the increase in population and wealth, they grew in size, equipments, and architectural design and finish. Few other sections of the country now have handsomer and more costly church edifices.

In influence and numbers the leading churches were the Methodist and the Baptist, and next to these came the Presbyterian. The ministers of these several sects were devout and zealous, some of them having ability of the highest order. With their fluency of speech, logical skill, and imaginative force, they were always popular and instructive, and often overpowering in their pulpit efforts. A few of the more brilliant were Randle, Wafer, Cravens, Parker, Slack, Ford, Bright, Haislip, Moreland, and Harris.[1]

In ideals, convictions, and habits the people were largely puritanic. Scarcely could a neighborhood be found in which dancing or card playing was practiced, and the observance of Sunday was almost universal.

Of course there were exceptions, even among the better classes. The author cannot vouch for the following story as to fact, but it is true as to conditions; that is, it might have been. The persons named were well known to the writer, and it was like them to have done as represented.

Brother John was a Georgian and a good Methodist, and Brother Ben was a South Carolinian and a good Baptist. They were neighbors and friends, witty and full of good humor, good shots and fond of hunting, and withal representatives of two of the best families of the country. With respect to the observance of Sunday they were alike in that "while the spirit was willing the flesh was weak," especially during the "gobbling-season."

One bright Sunday morning Brothers Ben and John were riding along a country road on their way to church. The dew glistened on the grass and the birds sang in every tree. There was a touch of springtime resurrection in the pure woodland air, and the bursting buds gave mute expression to the joy of life. A flock of wild turkeys was feeding in the woods, and, seeing the horsemen, struck a swinging trot and moved off like shadows to a near-by copse.

---

1. Rev. Harris was the father of the present brilliant State Superintendent of Education.

Brothers Ben and John at once became silent, sucked their pipes hard and sent forth, under much pressure, wisps of smoke into the air. "John," said Brother Ben finally, "it has just occurred to me that I left the cows in the pen, and I must return at once and let them out."

Now Brother John, being left alone, also returned, taking a different route. Soon afterwards, Brother Ben, having obtained his gun, was crawling along on his all-fours near where he had seen the turkeys, screening himself behind a large log in front of him. On reaching the log he heard a noise on the other side, and believing it to be caused by a turkey, peeped over; Brother John, also thinking that he was about to get a gobbler, peeped over from the other side, and the two gazed into each other's eyes.

Being surprised and somewhat abashed, both were silent for a moment, then broke into a hearty laugh. Brother John, with a merry twinkle in his eyes, took the other by the hand and said, "Brother Ben, let me congratulate you on joining the coterie of Louisiana gentlemen."

In the same jocular tone and spirit Brother Ben replied, "Brother John, every South Carolinian likes to associate with gentlemen; indeed, speaking reverently, in that upper and better world to which I hope we are all going, I really have less desire to sit with the angels than to stand among the gentlemen."

Introducing Oat

Life in North-Central Louisiana had its humorous as well as its serious side. Probably the wisest advice Dickens ever gave the world was to "keep jolly." He himself was a public benefactor in that he so often made the world laugh. It is well to grow to manhood or womanhood without losing a child's capacity for enjoyment, and this is what the people of that section largely did. One of the most familiar sounds in the house and on the farm, in the office or on the street, was hearty laughter. All classes seemed to be capable of joy without knowing the reason why. "Oh," once exclaimed a young lady, "I am just flooded with enthusiasm for – nobody knows what."

In such an atmosphere, as one would suppose, many wits and fun makers sprang up. Prominent among these was "Oat." As several of his jokes will be related in these chronicles, probably the reader would like to become somewhat acquainted with him at the outset. His real name is Oatis A. Smith. He was born in Dadeville, Alabama, and later resided in Gordon, Louisiana. He is a good citizen, and was a splendid soldier in the Civil War. He is witty, always sees the funny side of a situation, and enjoys a practical joke, whether he is the perpetrator or the victim.

Oat once went into the country to make some collections, and his trip led him into a region with which he was not familiar. There had been a great rainfall the night before, and the creeks and branches were swollen to inundation. He came to a wide expanse of water running across the road. Not knowing how deep it might be, and desiring to keep his shoes and socks dry, he alighted and pulled them off. He again mounted his horse, rode across safely, and was putting on his shoes when another man rode up and inquired, "How is it, neighbor?"

"Mighty bad," said Oat.

"What would you advise me to do?" asked the stranger.

"Do just what I did," said Oat. "Get off your horse, pull off all your clothes, shoes, and socks, tie them into a bundle with your suspenders, and ride across, holding the bundle high over your head."

"Well," said the fellow, "if I must I must," and he at once dismounted and began to "shuck" off his clothes.

In the meantime Oat, having dressed, mounted his horse and rode away. But when out of sight, he hid his horse in the bushes, and went back unseen to watch the performance.

The stranger followed the instructions with much regard for details. He mounted his horse, grasping its mane firmly with one hand, holding the bundle aloft with the other; and pressing his heels to the sides of the steed, he ventured into the "rolling deep." But imagine his joy and also his chagrin, when he discovered that the place had a hard, firm, sandy bottom, and the water was not more than ten inches deep.

Oat is now old in years but still young in buoyancy of spirits. That his love of jokes has not waned with the lapse of time is shown by the following incident, which occurred quite recently.

In the vicinity of Gordon, where Oat lives, there are a number of men and boys who are fond of hunting. They are good shots and pride themselves on their good marksmanship. These hunters often assemble at the village store, especially on a Saturday afternoon, bringing their guns and ammunition. Now Oat secured the skin of a squirrel, and had it nailed high up in a tall tree standing near the store. It was placed so that only small parts of the back and tail could be seen from any point of the grounds.

The following Saturday the hunters turned out in full force. An ally of Oat's looking quietly up the tall tree, his hands shading his eyes, said, "Boys, I do believe I see a squirrel up that tree."

One of the hunters, scanning the tree closely, said, "That

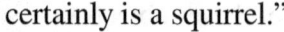

certainly is a squirrel."

The boys sprang instantly to their feet and made a rush for their guns, each anxious to secure the prize, and still more anxious to display his marksmanship.

One shot after another rent the air, and bark, twigs, and leaves fell, but no squirrel. Then volley after volley followed, filling the air with smoke and fragments of bark and twigs. But to the wonder of the boys the squirrel was as immovable as the Rock of Gibraltar.

"Boys," said one of the number, "that is the goldarn-dest squirrel I ever tackled."

Much powder and shot were wasted before it was found to be "one of Oat's tricks."

Homer College

Such was the boom in educational matters that the churches came to think that North-Central Louisiana needed and would support a college. So the following were founded: the Minden Female College, by the Presbyterians; the Mount Lebanon Male College, by the Baptists; and the Homer Male College, by the Methodists. These colleges had not as large or fine buildings as many of our present high schools; but at that time they were thought to be ample and grand. Some of these old buildings are still standing, and though out of style and repair, timeworn and weatherstained, they are splendid monuments to the high ideals of the men who founded them.

Although they had no funds, except those derived from tuition fees, they did well and in a certain sense were great schools. In the male colleges there was only one course of study, and that was made up chiefly of Latin, Greek, and Mathematics.

The teaching of these subjects does not require the costly equipments (apparatus, laboratory, shops, and so forth) that are needed to teach the many practical courses in our great colleges of to-day. This explains why they could be great schools without much means.

In those days people sent their sons to college to have their mental and moral natures trained, disciplined, and refined, with little thought as to how this culture could be turned to useful account, except in a general way. It was thought then that when a boy's mind was trained to think, compare, and reason he could easily learn the special things necessary to a lawyer, doctor, farmer, or any profession he might choose to follow. The following incident will illustrate their view of the matter:

In a certain town in Louisiana lived an eminent lawyer who, in conversation with a noted educator, said, "I have not the high appreciation of Latin, Greek, and Mathematics that I once had; I studied these things at the University of Virginia, but I have never had occasion to use them during my thirty years of experience as a lawyer."

Pointing to a brick wall on the opposite side of the street, the educator replied, "My dear sir, you know that in building that wall they used scaffolding; where is that scaffolding now? If that wall could speak, how foolish and how ungrateful it would be for it to say, 'I have no use for scaffolding; I have been standing here thirty years and I have never had occasion to use it during that long time.'"

"A great man once said," continued the educator, "if I should forget every fact and principle which I learned while at school and college I would not be a very poor man, but if I should lose the mental training which I acquired by the mastery of those facts I would be poor indeed."

Nick entered Homer College on its opening day. His mother went with him, and in presenting him to the faculty said, "Put him where you think he belongs; it is our purpose to keep him here until he graduates." Nick had been well prepared for college at the Forest Grove school. He stood the entrance examination and was assigned to the freshman class.

He was not examined in English, geography, or history; but mostly in Latin, arithmetic, and algebra. In Latin he had gone through the grammar, reader, Cicero, Cæsar, and the Æneid of Virgil. The best way to learn English was then thought to be through and by means of Latin; hence much of the English taught, especially rhetoric and belles-lettres, came late in the course of study, after the student had been well grounded in Latin.

There were no written tests as we have them today. When reciting, the class was seated on long benches in front of the teacher, and the students were quizzed or sent to the board one at a time, and were graded according to their answers. Examinations were public and conducted in the same way. The great assembly room of the college was often full of people on examination day, and one or more of the visitors, by request of the teacher, sometimes conducted the examination.

The citizens of Homer were often amused, and probably sometimes annoyed, by the pranks of the college boys. One Sunday morning as the people were quietly passing through the courthouse square on their way to church, some strange sights came into view. It looked as if all the business men had suddenly changed their places of business. A doctor's signboard was on a merchant's store, a saloon sign was on the post office, a lawyer's sign on a stable, the stable sign on the hotel, and so on. "That is the work of those mischievous college boys," said one of the party; and everybody smiled or laughed, thus confirming the statement of Haislip: "Man is the only creature that laughs, because he alone sees things as they are and as they should be."

At one time Dan Rice's circus was coming to town, and orders were issued prohibiting the college boys from attending. The faculty thought it hurtful to good morals to go to such places. Nevertheless a large number of the students went, thinking or hoping that it might not become known to the college authorities. But the president was alert; he learned of the violation, and suspended the participants, thirty-six in all, for a period of two weeks.

This outbreak, like many another prank of college life, was committed in mere wantonness of unexpended vitality. Probably it would not have happened had the pent up buoyancy of youth been relieved by some active duty or play. Many of those boys now sleep on the battlefields of the Civil War. Among the few still living the writer recalls Black,[1] John,[2] and Will,[3] all of whom have attained distinction or competency in their several lines of work.

Nick's roommate, Sam Pursley, always took a hand in any mischief that was going on. On the night of the circus he blacked himself with burnt cork, put on a ragged suit, and went to the show. Feeling that no one would see through his disguise, he mingled freely with all classes, and incited much amusement and laughter by his "Negro antics and lingo." Soon after that, Sam's father moved to Mississippi (in 1860), and the only time Nick and Sam ever saw each other again was during the last year of the Civil War (1865). Then they met and had a short talk on the road near Hamburg, South Carolina, Sam being in the cavalry and Nick in the infantry of the Confederate Army. Such are the strange coincidences of human life.

Nick and Hines[4] were college chums and in the same class. Hines was brilliant in Latin and Greek, and Nick was good

---

1. Judge W. F. Blackman, Alexandria, La.

2. John A. Traylor, Los Angeles, Cal.

3. Capt. W. A. Miller, Amarillo, Tex.

4. Hon. H. C. Mitchell, Homer, La.

in mathematics. Hence it took the two together to make one first-class student. Nick was a hard student of mathematics, incited and stimulated by a love rather than a talent for the subject. So he came to be dubbed the "college mathematician." The professor of mathematics once gave the class three days to solve a certain hard problem (the problem of "the three points" in trigonometry). He asked the class not to get any help or hints from the book or otherwise, and related such things about its use, history, and so forth, as to cause the boys to think it would be a great honor to the whole class if any one of them should solve it.

All eyes and hopes now turned to Nick, and to encourage him to do his best the boys promised him ever so many presents if he succeeded. "Nick," said Hines, "if you solve that problem I'll pay for your license when you get married." Well, to make a long story short, Nick solved the problem and received all the promised presents. Sixteen years after that he was married, and Hines, then a State senator, made good his promise also.

A strong feature of the college was the work of the two literary societies, in which a great deal of interest was taken by all the upper classmen. Indeed these societies, with their numerous, intelligent, and wealthy members, dominated the college in a large measure. Such was the trend of the times that the highest goal at which a college man could aim was to be a good speaker or orator. The course of study not only helped to awaken and foster this ideal, but it also trained the students in the means of its attainment. Therefore the societies prospered, and some of the members became good speakers in after life. In the month of May, 1861, the two societies met one Friday night for joint debate. Nick and Joe were appointed a committee to select the question to be discussed.[5] The Civil War had now begun, and

---

5. Joe and Nick were classmates, and chums both at college and in the war. In the bloody onslaught at Franklin, Tennessee, Joe, though severely wounded, could not be persuaded to leave the field. Nick, perceiving his suffering, approached him and said, "Joe, can I help you in any way?"

"No, Nick," said he, "I thank you; but as soon as you can I wish you would look after Colonel Nelson; I fear he is mortally wounded."

Such was ever his helpful and self-sacrificing disposition. Many

there was great excitement about it. One company, the "Claiborne Guards," had gone to the war, and there was talk of others going. So Nick and Joe agreed on this question:

"Resolved that the upper-classmen should resign from the college and go to the war."

The question was accepted and very ably debated on both sides. The affirmative won, and this served to arouse all the larger boys to action in the matter. There was little sleeping that night, but much earnest talking and planning. The next morning all the larger boys resigned from the college and went to their homes, expecting soon to go to the war.

---

years after the war the colonel of the regiment (the lamented T. C. Standifer), speaking of Joe to Nick said, "The South has no better citizen, nor had she a braver soldier."

CHAPTER SIX
The Story of the Beginning of the War
☆ ☆ ☆ ☆

The Irrepressible Conflict

When it became known that Mr. Lincoln had been elected President of the United States (November, 1860) there was great excitement all over the country. It is hard for one, at the present time, to realize how widely the North and the South had become separated in thought and feeling, especially with regard to certain leading questions and issues. It really seemed that an "irrepressible conflict" had arisen between them. So the Southern States, believing that the Union had become hurtful rather than helpful to their peace and welfare, resolved to withdraw from it, just as a partner would leave a business concern which had ceased to be pleasant and profitable to him. They seceded from the Union (annulled the compact which bound them to it), formed a government of their own, and called it the Confederate States of America.

Mr. Lincoln was an intense unionist; he believed and affirmed that the breaking up of the Union would be the greatest evil that could befall all the States. So he determined to preserve the Union at all hazards, and to this end sent an army into the South to quell the "rebellion."

How little the common people of the two sections really knew of one another – their thoughts, habits, characters, and ideals! This came from their living so far apart, and having no opportunity or means of mutual communication. Their knowledge of one another was based on hearsay, and this was distorted by partisans and fanatics. The South misjudged and undervalued the North in many ways, and evidently Mr. Lincoln himself had a poor idea of Southern conditions; for, to subdue the South, he called out 75,000 troops for three months, whereas as a matter of fact it took 9,750,000 soldiers four years to accomplish it. Had the common people North and South known each other better – their patriotism, devotion to the Union, and ideals of right and wrong – probably their differences would have been healed without the cost of so much blood and treasure.

Nick Goes to War

It was on a superb spring morning that Nick, with his gun and dog, was strolling through the dark green woods near his father's country home. What lad would not have been happy under the same conditions! For him there had just been substituted outdoor freedom for indoor restraints, hunting for studying, the songs of birds and the murmur of running water for a stillness unrelieved except by the rattle of chalk or the clatter of slate pencils. No sound or sight of the landscape evaded the lad's quickened and responsive senses. A buttercup quivered and bowed under the flutter and weight of a bee extracting its honey; a "news-carrier" (syrphus fly), just arrived from fairyland, poised in mid air and cheered the boy with its fanciful message; a sapsucker flopped from a distant tree to one nearby and ran in dismal spirals about one of its big branches. All nature was "laughing in the madness of joy"; never seemed the sky so blue, the foliage so green, nor the odor of the honeysuckle so sweet.

It is dreadful how quickly a delightful situation may be changed. Over the hills came the long swelling blasts of Uncle Wash's hunting horn. Nick knew at once that it was a call to him to come home. He struck a bee line for the house, feeling that it must be something about the war, for people now thought and talked of little else. At the front gate he met his cousin Billie,[1] who

---

1. W.C. Boring, Shreveport, La.

lived in the western part of the parish. He was also a lusty lad, a little older than Nick, and strong enough to handle a pike. Turning on Nick a cheerful, ruddy face, he said, "Nick, we are making up a company to go to the war, and I came all the way over here to get you to join it. It is nearly made up, and you will have to apply soon to get your name on the roll."

Before replying Nick glanced at his mother. Though her lips were smiling, she looked at him out of deep, sad eyes with no glint of mirth in them. "My son," said she, "you have my consent to go, if you so desire." There was a look of anxiety in her clear gray eyes as she added, "This is going to be a more serious affair than our people appear to think; but go, and may God be with you." At the time Nick scarcely heeded the expression, but often since he has wondered if it was one of fear or a vision.

The next day (Sunday) Nick saw his friend Oat, and told him of his purpose to go with Billie to the war. "Nick," said Oat in his usual jesting tone and manner, "you and Bill will need a guardian, if not a nurse; so I reckon I'd better go along with you." That same day, late in the afternoon, Oat and Nick started on a twenty-five-mile ride, so anxious were they to get their names on the roll. Their route led through Homer.

With their start also appeared the signs of an approaching tempest. Soon lowering clouds began to chase one another as if mad. The darkness of the night increased as the heavens became more overcast. After a while the fitful flashes of lightning alone revealed the surroundings of the riders, while loud peals of thunder shook the earth and reverberated over their heads. Just as they reached the college large drops of rain began to fall. They stopped, hitched their mules, and with their saddles and blankets made pallets on the floor of the college hall. Lying on these rough beds and lulled by the roar of wind and rain, they fell asleep. What an experience – the ride, the storm, the bed! What a fitting introduction to the career of the Dixie soldier! Was it an accident or a harbinger? God only knows.

After a sound two-hour nap they mounted their mules, continued their journey, and had the joy and honor of being enrolled as members of the "Claiborne Rangers," of which Thomas M. Scott was captain.

The first day of July, 1861, was fixed as the time for the company to assemble in Homer and start to the war. These were now busy and exciting times. Every soldier was to have a uniform – a roundabout coat with large horn buttons – and all the ladies joined in to help make them. The ladies met in groups at different places and there was a great deal of planning, measuring, sewing, and chattering. The young people lived in a fever of excitement. Uncle Wash made Nick a great bowie knife that was nearly a foot long. On the night before the day of departure, Nick was so wrought up in mind that he could scarcely go to sleep. He rose early the next morning, put on his uniform and also his belt, to which was attached a scabbard carrying his big knife. "Ah," thought he, "Mr. Yank had better keep out of my way." His little sister dashed into her mother's room and exclaimed, "Mama, Nick looks like the picture of Jack the Giant Killer."

Homer was full of people on the first of July. They had come in wagons, in buggies, and on horseback from all parts of the parish. Mothers were there to kiss their sons good-by, and pretty girls were there to bid their sweethearts farewell. Drums were beating, bands playing, and flags waving. The boys looked fine and grand in their new uniforms, though scarcely any two of the suits were exactly alike. With their pistols and bowie knives they had quite a warlike air, and a few must bluster some to show their manhood. "Good morning, Henry," said Miss Mary to a friend; "you are just splendid as a soldier;" and Henry would clear his throat and square his shoulders as a real soldier does when commended for valor.

With a few exceptions all felt and acted as if they were

going to a picnic. It was commonly believed that the war would not last long. This belief was simply a part of the natural optimism of the people. Nick almost prayed that the war would not close before he got into one battle; but after he got into one he then prayed that it would close before he got into another.

It was sixty miles to the nearest railroad. This distance was to be traveled by the Claiborne Rangers in wagons or on foot. They knew nothing of drilling; this was the first time many of them had ever seen one another. But few had even heard of "fall in." So there was no attempt to form or march them in military order. When they started every fellow went as he pleased.

When the order was given to march there was much cheering and shaking of hands, and good wishes were showered upon the departing soldiers. Oat said it was really a relief when they had gone so far that friends and relatives could no longer say to them "good-by" and "God bless you." The poor fellows did not dream that many a long day was to pass before they again saw faces so beaming with looks of love and good will. With Aunt Martha's last embrace of Nick there came a far-away, dreamy look into her eyes. She was staring at him, but he felt himself almost outside the range of her vision. Nick never forgot that look, piercing as it were the realms of the future, and in after years wondered if she then had a premonition of her own passing away before his return from the war. While her beautiful eyes bespoke fear, anxiety, and sorrow, there was no dimming of the indomitable light that lived in their clear depths.

There were enough wagons and hacks to haul the entire party, their baskets of food, and their luggage. Some of the men rode and others walked, and when tired of the one they did the other. All along the road, people cheered them with their smiles, kind words, and good wishes, the men waving their hats and the women their handkerchiefs.

Late in the afternoon they reached the Gee Place, and there they pitched camp for the night. Most of the men had been on camp hunts and camp fishings, and were more or less familiar with camp life. They knew what to do and how to do it to make themselves quite comfortable. There was a great stir and bustle in feeding and watering the stock, preparing and eating supper, and making pallets of blankets and comforts. After that the men became more quiet; they sat in groups on logs or pallets and told stories, cracked jokes, and sang familiar songs. As the night wore away they went by ones or twos "to bed," until none were left. On their rude couches they slept as soundly and as sweetly as if they had been in their soft beds at home. While they slumbered, the stars shone brightly in the skies as if keeping watch over them, and the stillness of the night was broken only by the whip-poorwill as in the deep shadows of the forest, it poured forth its plaintive call, "chuck, will-widow."

The men rose early the next morning, fed the stock, prepared and ate breakfast, and continued the march. The scenes and events along the road did not differ much from those of the day before. One mile west of Vienna they passed the old Wafer Place, the home of Nick's maternal great-grandfather. The second night they camped at the "Gum Spring," and the third night, in the courthouse yard of the beautiful city of Monroe.

A new railroad ran from Monroe to Vicksburg, and this was the first one many of the Rangers had ever seen. Some platform cars were provided with seats made of rough planks, and on these the soldiers were transported from Monroe to Vicksburg. The terminal of the road at that time was DeSoto, a small village just across the river from Vicksburg. It has long since been destroyed by the changes in the channel of the great river. From DeSoto they were ferried across the river to Vicksburg. Here they stopped a few hours, during which time Nick went to an art gallery and had his "ambrotype" taken, a copy of which faces this page.

From Vicksburg the company went by rail to Jackson, Mississippi, and thence journeyed to Camp Moore, Louisiana.

Nick as a soldier

Camp Moore

In the piny woods of Tangipahoa Parish there is a certain old field neglected and overgrown with pine bushes. Thousands have seen it from the passing trains of the Illinois Central without suspecting that it was the site of a great military encampment in the stormy days of '61. Here Camp Moore, named after the governor of Louisiana, was located. Hardly could a more appropriate place for the purpose have been found – seventy-five miles from New Orleans, sufficiently rolling for easy drainage, and level enough for military evolutions. Situated as it was in the ozone belt, the air was pure and sweet, and redolent with the odor of fresh pine straw. On one side was Beaver Creek and on the other the Tangipahoa River, both running streams of clear sparkling water.

Here the sons of Louisiana went to enlist in the army and to be trained in the duties of soldiers. When the war began these sons knew nothing of drilling, guard mounting, and many other duties which alone make men efficient in the camp and on the march and the battle field. Camp Moore was established by the State to provide this instruction. In a word, it was a real military school in which men were trained for war and formed into battalions and regiments. In this school they were kept usually six or eight weeks and then forwarded to the "front," where the fighting was to be done.

As green and awkward as the Claiborne boys were with respect to drilling, there were three things in military life they could do as well as the drill master: shoot quick and straight, put up tents, and march in "route-step" (go as you please). They marched in this go-as-you-please style from the depot to the camp, – a large drill-ground in front of "a little city of white tents." The grounds were as smooth as a floor and as clean as a newly swept yard, and the white tents were arranged in straight parallel rows. Everything seemed to have been designed and finished with a single eye to order and cleanliness. Here and there on the campus were squads of soldiers, each being drilled by an officer who was as straight as an Indian and as "bossy as a new overseer." "Shoulder arms!" "Forward, guide right, march!" "Company, left half wheel, march!" The welkin rang with these and other commands, each having something of the clear crack of a rifle.

When the Rangers received their tents they at once put them up in two rows, facing one another, and Captain Scott said, "They look as well as any on the grounds." The next day officers were elected, and the company mustered into service for one year. Then they drew guns – all kinds, scarcely any dozen of them being of the same pattern. Thus equipped, they entered upon all the duties of soldiers; namely, drilling, guard mounting every morning, dress parade every afternoon, policing, inspections, cleaning quarters, washing clothes, drawing rations, cooking and eating the frugal meals.

When a regiment was formed and sent to the "front" its place was soon filled by new companies coming in from all parts of the State. A few of these were Irish, more French, and still more English. Ten of the English companies from North-Central Louisiana, including the Claiborne Rangers, were formed into a regiment, known as the 12th Regiment, Louisiana Infantry. Of this regiment Captain Scott, of the Rangers, was elected Colonel.

The 12th was formed of a thousand young men – stalwart, muscular, dauntless hobbledehoys. They were the sons of lawyers, doctors, business men, and farmers, and having been reared largely in Christian homes they had that pride and morale which make men towers of strength in peace and in war. Of course their military potency could not be estimated before training and trial, but there was the assurance in advance that "blood will tell"; for there flowed in their veins the blood of the heroes of Hastings and Marston Moor, Valley Forge and Yorktown, Horse Shoe Bend and New Orleans, Buena Vista and Chapultepec.

It was a short walk from camp to the Tangipahoa River, and early in the morning and late in the afternoon the soldiers were permitted to go there to bathe and swim. This was much enjoyed by all, and every day the river was lined with the jolly and noisy swimmers. Indeed, throughout the war, the range of their pleasures being so narrow, the men went in the creeks, mill ponds, and rivers whenever they had a chance, even in pretty cold weather, that being about their only pastime. They often took their soiled clothes, washed them, and spread them on the bushes to dry, while they bathed and played in the water.

It was at Camp Moore that Nick learned to swim. That was queer, for, as a rule, Louisiana boys take to water almost as soon as they can walk. But after that, Nick made up for lost time by swimming in, if not across, nearly every stream between that place and the Atlantic Ocean.

When the men neglected duty or violated the rules they were punished in severe and singular ways. A soldier once stole something, and was punished for it by having to wear a board fastened to his back on which was printed ROGUE. Often a culprit was punished by having to wear a barrel, or being tied up by the thumbs, or put in stocks or a pillory.

As a rule, it was only the rowdies who had to be treated in this way. The men generally did their duties cheerfully and faithfully. As the war progressed the roughs, rowdies, and bullies gradually "played out." It is men of moral courage that make dependable and enduring soldiers. Hence punishments became fewer as the war went on.

There was an Irishman in the 11th regiment named Kelly, who was punished for drunkenness by being put under guard with a chain and ball attached to his ankle. Kelly had been a steamboat roustabout, and was a giant in size and strength. Nick happened to be on guard that day and had to guard Kelly. Now the big Irishman, moved by a spirit of humor or desperation, seemed to be watching for a chance to spring on Nick and beat the life out of him. So every time he moved down would come Nick's gun. It was loaded with an ounce ball and Kelly knew it. When the corporal of the guard came, Kelly said to him in a whisper: "Would ye be after putting a man in the place of that spalpeen of a lad? The little cuss has got so he won't let me turn over."

Nick was as glad to go as Kelly was to have him go.

Exposure and other causes produced much sickness among the troops. At the beginning of the war each camp was supplied with a hospital in which the sick were cared for. In it were clean beds, medicines, and nurses, and many ladies came with flowers and delicacies for the patients. But year by year, as the war went on, camp hospitals became poorer and the medicines scarcer, until they really disappeared altogether. At first the chief kind of sickness was measles, which is usually a harmless disease, but a very fatal one when the subject is exposed. More men died of it during the war than of all other diseases together. It caused the death of more than a dozen of the Claiborne Rangers at Camp Moore.

Many of the bodies of deceased soldiers were taken to their homes for burial, and the rest were interred on a mound in the woods nearby. The latter were buried with military honors; that is, the remains were escorted to the graveyard by a squad of soldiers, and when the body was put in the ground the squad fired three rounds of blank cartridges over the grave. It was a very sad and impressive service.

The site of Camp Moore is now an old and deserted field. All signs of the camp are gone. There is nothing left to remind one of the stirring scenes of '61. Instead of the merry laugh and heavy tramp of soldiers, one now hears the "mournful song" of the pine straw as it is swept by the passing breeze.

Many years after the war the Daughters of the Confederacy induced the legislature to appropriate enough money to buy the old graveyard, clean it off, build a strong iron fence around it, and erect a monument in memory of the men, living and dead, who served there. When the monument was unveiled (1907) Nick, then a professor in the State university, made the dedication speech.

Two large beech trees were left standing in the inclosure on account of the many names of the soldiers cut into their bark. Among these old carvings Nick's attention was called to his own initials, "J. W. N.," which were probably cut by him just forty-six years before.

In the latter part of August the 12th was ordered to "the front." With what a thrill of excitement was the order received by the men! At last their hopes of getting into a battle were to be realized! Up to this time they had had no news to write home except the details of camp life. Now they were to go far away into Kentucky, where the storm of war would soon be raging.

There was a great hurry and bustle in preparing to move – taking down tents, packing luggage, and cooking three days' rations. When they boarded the train each man carried a knapsack, a haversack, a canteen, two blankets, and a gun and cartridge box. It was a long freight train that was to carry them, and some took passage in and some on top of the box cars. When it "pulled out" a long and loud hurrah was shouted by a thousand jolly fellows. Poor boys! They little dreamed of the hardships and privations in store for them.

It is not the intention of this book to give any account of the battles and conflicts of the War between the States. As to how the Dixie boys acquitted themselves as soldiers is briefly told in the following tribute to them by General Early:

"I believe the world has never produced a body of men

superior, in courage, patriotism, and endurance, to the private soldiers of the Confederate armies. I have repeatedly seen those soldiers submit with cheerfulness to privations and hardships which would appear to be almost incredible; and the wild cheers of these brave men when their lines sent back the opposing host of Federal troops, staggering, reeling, and flying, have often thrilled every fibre in my heart. I have seen, with my own eyes, ragged, barefooted, and hungry Confederate soldiers perform deeds, which, if performed in days of yore, by mailed warriors in glittering armor, would have inspired the harp of the minstrel and the pen of the poet."

CHAPTER SEVEN
The Story of Events of the War
☆ ☆ ☆ ☆

Minor Incidents

Many things occur in wars of which history makes no mention. As a rule, it tells of the greater and not of the smaller events. Yet the latter are the happenings that young people like most to hear about. Stories of little incidents of the camp, the march, and the battle not only make pleasant reading, but give one a good idea of the temper of the soldiers and the kind of men they were.

The idea of war which one gets from history is that it is a series of severe ills and toils. This is true, and probably no soldiers ever realized it more keenly than the Confederates during the War between the States. Yet old soldiers say they had as many hearty laughs during that war as they ever had in any other four years of their lives. So war must have something of an amusing as well as a serious side. Fortunate is the soldier who has the "saving grace of humor" through and by which this funny side is discernible.

Few armies have had a greater number of wits than the Confederate. However tired, hungry, and thirsty the men might be, however long the march, or hard the battle, or gloomy the outlook, some one would see the "funny side" of it, and so express it as to put the others to smiling if not laughing. No doubt this reviving and stimulating of the spirits and morale of the men went far to supply the want of food and medicine. Indeed, it is believed that this merriment had much to do in making the Dixie boys the splendid soldiers they were enabling them to prolong the struggle against such great odds and with such scanty means.

A regiment was once passing through a small village. The men had been marching and fighting, more or less, for several days. They were not only tired, thirsty, and hungry, but their backs were chafed by the straps which supported their cartridge boxes, canteens, and haversacks. It was a hot summer day, and the only noise that broke the silence in ranks was the heavy grinding of the men's feet as they pulled their way through the deep dry sand.

As they passed near a church where a Negro was tolling the bell one of the men, in a husky voice, inquired, "Hello, boy; what are you ringing that bell for?"

"Somebody dead," said the Negro.

"Well," said the soldier, "strike her a few licks for me, for I'm nearly dead."

Weary and worn, with the prospect of a fight just ahead of them, some Confederate soldiers were passing a cotton factory in North Carolina. One of the men, glancing at the lofty stack chimney, exclaimed, "I wonder how they ever built that tall chimney?"

"I can tell you," replied Jim[1]; "they first built the hole in it and then built the chimney around the hole."

---

1. James Bernard.

After a hard day's march a regiment pitched camp near a small village. Soon a Negro boy entered the camp with a note from the young ladies of the village inviting "the young men of the regiment" to a dance that evening. The boys at once got busy, washing off their old shoes, patching and brushing their coats and trousers, and pulling the tangles out of their hair with curry combs.

On going into the dance hall the boys found the girls assembled at one end of the room, and they soon gathered at the other end. And there they were with no one to introduce them.

At last one of the fellows walked up to a pretty girl and, with a smile in his eyes, very gallantly asked, "Miss, may I have the first dance with you?"

Very gracefully she said, "Why, I don't know you."

"Well," said he, "you don't take any more chances than I do."

General Richard Taylor entered the Confederate Army as colonel of a regiment made up almost entirely of French boys from South Louisiana. Upon reaching Richmond he was ordered to report to General Stonewall Jackson. Taylor found the redoubtable Stonewall sitting on a fence and sucking a lemon. The regiment halted, stacked arms, and disbanded. Then the band struck up a lively tune, and the gay Creoles, although having just finished a long and hard march, paired off and began a jolly dance.

"Very gay men for serious work," said Stonewall to Taylor.

"I hope they will be none the less good soldiers on account of their gayety," said the colonel.

General Jackson shook his head as if he thought, "I don't see how that can be."

Whereupon Colonel Taylor is reported to have said, "General Jackson, French soldiers, just such as these, have whipped the men and kissed the women all over the world."

One dark night Ben[2] stumbled up to a dim firelight around which a number of soldiers were standing, sitting, or lying. The darkness was intense, it being both a cloudy and a moonless night.

"Boys," said Ben, "I met the blackest Negro awhile ago I ever saw.

"Bah, Ben," exclaimed one of the men; "how could you see a Negro or anything else in such pitch-darkness as this?"

"I saw him," said Ben, "by the very absence of his color; he was so black he looked like a hole, in the darkness."

A Fish Story

When one begins to tell a fish story the listener is apt to think, "Whatever you say will sound like a lie; so it doesn't really matter." In the present instance the facts are at least less exaggerated than in the old story where "they bit so fast one had to stand behind a tree to bait his hook."

On May 15, 1863, the 12th was camped on the Big Black River just above the point where it is crossed by the railroad running from Vicksburg through Jackson, Mississippi. The immense army under Gen. Grant, having effected a landing at Grand Gulf, and forced its way through the interior to Jackson, was now faced toward the west, and slowly investing the Confederate forces under Gen. Pemberton. A great battle was drawing near in which the Dixie Army would either have to cut its way through the much larger army of Gen. Grant or be driven back into the intrenchments of Vicksburg.

At this critical moment an event occurred which shows how little the Dixie boys were disposed to brood over coming troubles and impending disasters. About a mile from the camp of the 12th were a number of lagoons, and on the morning of the 15th it became known that these abounded in fish, large and small. How this discovery was made by the men is not known. It

---

2. B.F. Sikes, Texas.

is wonderful what news-gatherers they were, especially in reference to "grub." Soon the way to the lagoons was crowded with the would-be fishermen. Never had they gone to a picnic with more exhilarating zest, nor did they ever charge the "Yankees" with grimmer determination.

The lakelets were found to be about fifty feet wide and three feet deep. The question at once arose as to how the fish might be caught. The boys had no fishing tackle – lines, hooks, seines, or gigs. But here, as in many other cases, necessity was the mother of invention. Some one suggested how "seines" might be made of vines; viz., get a long vine and wrap it with other vines, thus forming a roll some fifty feet long, three feet thick in the middle, and tapering to points at the ends. There were plenty of vines in the swamp, plenty of men to do the work, and the only necessary tools were pocket knives. Soon the woods were alive with the hum of industry and a new manufactory in process of operation.

The moment a seine was finished it was seized by a score of lusty fellows, who, stripped of their clothes, dragged it into the lagoon, and pushed or pulled it across, from side to side, just as an ordinary seine would have been used. With the seine pressed hard against the bottom of the lakelet, the openings between the vines being too small to allow the passage of large fish through them, there were landed at each haul a number of buffalo and catfish, and along with these were often one or more turtles and moccasins. The boys entered into the sport with zest of picnickers. They continued to seine "hole" after "hole," as long as there was a prospect for more fish and more fun.

At last they started

to camp, carrying many buffalo fish weighing from one to three pounds. So covered were they with black sticky mud that the identity of each and all was destroyed except for his form and voice. Before reaching camps they went to the river to wash themselves and the fish. Scarcely had they done this "next-to-Godly" act when the "long roll" called them to "fall in." The regiment was soon on the march, many of the men having one or more buffaloes dangling from their haversacks.

It was a hot day, and the fish became "heavier and heavier"; so, one by one, they were dropped by the roadside, until the entire catch was strewn along the road for a distance of probably ten miles. That night, after a long and hard march, the regiment "slept on arms" in a cornfield. The next day, May 16, the battle of Baker's Creek, or Champion Hill, was fought, into which the fishermen entered as actively, though not as pleasantly, as in the fishing frolic of the day before. At the first roll call after the battle there were many vacant places in the ranks – some of the fishermen too had fallen. Brave, noble boys! May your ashes rest in peace, is the prayer of one of the few surviving seiners.

A Confederate Scout

Of the boys who attended the old Forest Grove school, already described, none could run faster and longer or jump further and higher than Wafe.[3] He was not much of a bookworm, but in athletics, hilarity, and mischief he led the school – always played deer in the "game of deer," and always knew every boy's speech except his own. Good-natured, generous, and courageous, yet he was a genius in devising mischief and getting other boys into awkward, embarrassing, and scary situations. It is queer how he maintained his popularity with all classes – was liked even by the victims of his roughest jokes. As a rider and shot a Texas Ranger was not more daring or skillful.

Wafe was the brother of Syranus, of whom a story is told later on, and he (Wafe) is the father of Chappell, a recent graduate of Tulane University, who was widely known in college cir-

---

3. H. W. Menefree, Homer, La.

cles as one of the greatest all-round athletes the South has produced. How queerly heredity works! In many particulars the brothers were as dissimilar as the father and son are alike.

When the war broke out Wafe enlisted and served in the cavalry. Upon the fall of Vicksburg General Johnston, commanding the Confederate forces, fell back to Jackson, and was pursued by General Sherman, commanding a corps of the Federal Army. After a severe encounter at Jackson, Johnston retreated to Newton Station, and was again followed by Sherman.

Now the Confederate leader, desiring to know whether or not his antagonist intended to pursue him farther across the country, determined to send a scout around Sherman's army to ascertain, among other things, the size of his wagon train. To this end he instructed the commander of the cavalry to send him an efficient trooper, – a cavalier of tried courage, sagacity, and reliability. Wafe was at once selected and ordered to report to General Johnston.

Some of Wafe's close friends learned of the project, and in discussing the perilous adventure Joe[4] said, "Well, if Wafe is provided with a good horse he'll come out all right."

Billie, who had chased Wafe in many a "game of deer," thus replied, "In any case of emergency, whether he has a horse or not, if he can only get a fair start I defy the whole Yankee army to catch him."

Without going into details, suffice it to say Wafe made the circuit, and discharged the service with consummate tact and daring. Venturing into critical positions in order to get full and accurate information, he had several hairbreadth escapes.

Returning, he made his report to General Johnston, who correctly divined from it that Sherman would push the invasion no further, and so notified the President of the Confederacy. Tak-

---

4. Maj. J.W. Boring, Longview, Tex.

ing Wafe by the hand he said: "I congratulate you on the success of your mission, and thank you for your valuable services."

Wafe is still living, hale and healthy. While he is not so great a tease as in the olden times, yet Nick would not now "go in swimming" with him without some assurance that Wafe would not "duck" him.

Stories of Oat

This is not the first time the reader has heard of Oat, one of Nick's close and lifelong friends. Once when the 12th was camped near Grenada, Mississippi, the colonel sent for Nick and Oat and said, "Nick, I wish you and Oat to go to Jackson to obtain some clothing and blankets for the regiment. You can leave on the train this afternoon, which will put you in Jackson about eleven to-night."

In handing them their permits and orders for the supplies he added, "Now, you men will have to be very careful in Jackson as to where you go, for the smallpox is said to be raging in all parts of the city."

When Oat and Nick reached Jackson it was very dark, cold, and rainy. There were no hotels or boarding houses to go to, so they at once set out to find some kind of shelter that would at least protect them from the rain. After strolling around in the darkness for some time they came upon an old rickety box car standing on a sidetrack.

"This will do," said Oat.

They grasped the heavy shutter of the door and were sliding it back, when some one within shouted, "Who's that?"

"Two soldiers looking for shelter," replied Oat. "You had better stay out of here," said the voice within; "there are two cases of smallpox in here."

"That's all right," said Oat; "we've got the smallpox too."

"The devil you say! Well – you fellows stand aside till we get out."

So Oat and Nick stood aside; the fellows within crawled out and scampered off to parts unknown.

As they stretched out on their hard and lonely couch Oat said, "Nick, the greatest thing in this world is bluff; it has more to do with a man's success, in peace and in war, than any other one thing."

As a rule, the Dixie soldiers were always hungry – at least hungry for some "good old home-cooked food." Citizens living near a camp of soldiers, being so often called upon by the troops for one favor or another, especially food, were so stripped of everything that they had less and less to give, and less and less disposition to do so. One day Oat and Nick walked far into the interior, hoping to secure a good meal at some remote place that had not been annoyed and "eaten out" by the soldiers.

Stopping in front of a house, Nick said, "Now, Oat, you do the talking."

In response to Oat's loud "Hello" a lady came out on the front gallery, and the "gallant soldiers" bowed very low to her, wishing her to know how much better their manners were than their garments.

"Madam," said Oat, "we are so hungry we feel as if we were hollow from our mouths to our feet. Can't you let us have something to eat?"

"My friends," said the lady, "there is nothing cooked on this place, and there is very little to cook. We women have a hard time trying to make a living with our sons and husbands in the war. Truly, if I had it I would divide the last morsel with you."

"Madam," said Oat, "we believe you, and wish we had the means of helping you. Please pardon us for this intrusion. Good-by."

The two soldiers raised their hats, and were walking quietly away, when the lady said, "My friends, I have a large quantity of fine peaches which I have just picked for drying purposes. If you like good peaches, and will come in, you may have all you wish."

In a moment Oat and Nick were in the house. They found one of the rooms to be full of large cotton baskets, and each of these was filled with choice peaches. Following a suggestion of the lady it did not take the boys long to slide a basket out into the hall, take their seats by it, and begin to eat. Truly, as Oat said subsequently, they "laid up for the future as a camel does for the desert journey; peaches passed from sight under their manipulations as eggs do in a sleight of hand performance."

"Now, gentlemen," said the lady, "some of those peaches are very fine; look over them and select the best."

Then Oat, laying down his knife, looking and speaking very earnestly, and as if to relieve her of all anxiety in the matter, said, "My dear madam, it don't really make any difference 'cause we are going to eat 'em all anyhow."

General John B. Gordon told a good story of a soldier in his old regiment whose leg was so shattered by the fragment of a bomb that it had to be amputated. He was discharged from the army and went home. But as soon as he was able to walk with the aid of crutches he returned to the army and reënlisted, determined to help the cause in any way he could. One night, shortly after his return, he attended a prayer meeting. The chaplain led the services, and in his prayer he implored, "O Lord, give our men more zeal, more courage, more fortitude, and —"

Just here he was interrupted by the one-legged soldier, who said, "Ah, parson, you've got that all wrong; we have a plenty of all that; what we want you to pray for is more ammunition and provisions; let Him give us these and we'll attend to all the rest."

Not many soldiers in ancient or modern times ever did more hard service, and on such meager supplies, than the Confederates. Throughout many a long campaign they had not a change of clothes. The same coats, trousers, and shoes were worn summer and winter, and one can well imagine how thin and ragged they became. During the last two years of the war there were no tents, and the only means the men had of protecting themselves from rain and cold was the few blankets they could pack.

The main cooking vessels were frying pans and light camp kettles, and these the men often carried by hand or suspended to their belts. The usual food was corn bread, made of unsifted meal, about a half ration of poor beef, and red pepper, of which latter there was always plenty. When the pones of bread became hard and dry, as they did when two or three days old, they were soaked in water, cooked into mush, and seasoned with red pepper. This choice (?) dish was called "cush." The men were usually so hungry that to them cush was real good food. Nick often thought, "If I ever get home I am going to have Aunt Kitty to cook me as much cush as I want."

During the Tennessee campaign under General Hood the army suffered very much from toil, cold, and hunger. Once, while on the retreat, Nick was trudging along with the remnant of the 12th, and wondering if he could find some waste grains of corn where horses had been fed. Jim coming in from the rear, put his hand on Nick's shoulder and asked him in a whisper, "Nick, do you like chicken pie?"

Nick was at once interested, thinking or hoping that maybe Jim10 had somewhere and somehow obtained some of that good old Georgia dish. With an intense anxiety he asked also in a whisper, "Jim, tell me truly, why do you ask that?" "Well," quietly replied Jim, "I didn't think you did, for I never see you eating any."

An Interrupted Oration

Some men are cut out for one thing and some for another. A great lawyer might have made a poor mechanic and a good farmer an indifferent surgeon. That a man is unequal to a certain duty or office is often no reflection on his gifts; probably he is far superior intellectually to him who is so fitted. One can hardly think of a greater misfit than Charles J. Fox or Lord Byron as a commander and trainer of a military company. Every old soldier of any war knows that leadership in social and civil life is no assurance of leadership in military life; and vice versa.

In the Southern army were many brilliant young men who had been reared in wealthy and cultured homes, and educated in the best schools of the country – high livers and good fellows every inch of them, thoroughly at home in the parlor, on the rostrum, and in the salons of fashionable circles, and everywhere racy, charming, and without vanity. Yet many of them never attained to military rank or distinction, partly because they were not fitted by habits or temperament for office, but mostly because they cared but little, if at all, for it. They regarded office, in its lower aspects, somewhat as they did that of overseer on their father's plantation. To be first among equals they considered worth while, but power and command over the masses was to them "the tawdry eminence that bosses crave and shallow snobbish people admire." To them the petty detail of the service was drudgery and its pomp and show mummery. The battle, especially a dashing and hazardous charge, was the one thing which broke the monotony and into which they entered with gusto, if not with thrilling delight.

One of these cultured, rollicking fellows was Syranus[5] – handsome, graceful, and full of laughter, song and story. He had at least one weakness – a weakness then common to all of his kind: he sometimes drank too much "booze" and became tipsy. When in this "happy state" his first and main thought was to make a speech.

During the "hundred-days fight" from Dalton to Atlanta, Syranus was on detail in the commissary department, and for the time took no part in the fighting except when he slipped away to participate in a battle. This he did now and then, being a good

---

5. S.W. Menefree, Cotton Valley, Ala.

mixture of the fighter and the dreamer. One day he got some "Louisiana rum," became tipsy, and made his way to the front where the men were stationed behind a high breastwork. It was near Marietta, Georgia.

"Boys," said he, addressing mainly his old friends, "I came out here – hic – to make a speech – hic – to those Yankees over there in front of the works – hic – and my purpose is to bring this crazy war to a close – hic —"

His friends, thinking it all swagger, paid but little attention to him and less to his silly proposition. Almost unnoticed by them he mounted the breastwork and in a clear, ringing voice began:

"Gentlemen of the United States, – hic – I respectfully ask your earnest attention for a few moments. – hic – My purpose is to pave the way to the closing of this cruel war. – hic – I would assure you on the honor of a gentleman – hic – that it is quite a different thing to live in Boston and gossip of raids into the South and to live in the South and experience them. – hic —"

Two of his cousins, Joe[6] and Billie,[7] knowing the great danger he was in, seized him by the legs and were about to pull him off the works, when he turned his back to the front and said, "Now, boys, I insist that you permit me to go on; I know what I'm doing – hic –, and —"

"Bang," went a gun out in front, and "whack," the ball hit Syranus in the back.

It then took no more coaxing or pulling to get him off the works; the speech and also the drunk were brought to a sudden close.

Fortunately Syranus was wearing a belt, and still more fortunately the ball struck it and, hitting it a glancing blow, in-

---

6. Capt. J.F. Taylor, Amarillo, Tex.

7. W.C. Boring, Shreveport. La.

flicted only a severe bruise. The next morning Joe[8] and Nick, both cousins of Syranus, called to see him.

"Syranus," said Joe, "what could have possessed you to do a thing so silly and foolhardy?"

"Joe," replied Syranus, "drink not only blunts my sense of fear but inclines me to give expression to my most serious thoughts. Lately I have been brooding over the silliness, incongruities, and injustice of this war, and I suppose it was of that that I desired to speak."

"Tell us," said Nick, "just what you mean by all that."

"Well, briefly, it is this: at least half of the men in the Southern Army, although fighting in a way for secession, do not believe in it. Indeed, they made the political fight of their lives to defeat it.

"Again, as you are aware, a large proportion of the slave owners of the South, including all our kith and kin and such representative men as Judge McGehee,[9] are in favor of freeing the Negroes, provided it be done by the plan of 'gradual emancipation.' By that method the Negroes could be prepared for freedom, and in the meantime the South could work out of the labor system in and by which all her agricultural, commercial, and educational ways and means have been molded and operated for generations.

"Furthermore, that humane and rational method of freeing the Negroes would conserve the kind and sympathetic relation which, in general, has always existed between the two races in the South. In any event, the singular situation is that we are fighting to break up the Union and perpetuate slavery, when we are in a way opposed to both these projects."

"If the partisans and fanatics," continued he, "could have been set aside and the common people, North and South, could have been brought into a free and full conference over the questions at issue, I believe the Union could have been preserved and that the Negroes could have been freed without any war. But this,

---

8. Maj. J.W. Boring, Longview, Tex.

9. Judge McGehee probably had more slaves than any man in the South.

I suppose, was impracticable and therefore impossible. One thing, however, is very clear to my mind and that is, the Federal Government should at least have tried to follow the example set by Great Britain in freeing her slaves – buy them and set them free."

"It seems to me," continued he, "that such a course was recommended by every consideration of justice, equity, and law. Evidently the North and the South were alike responsible for the 'institution of slavery' in this country; the 'system' grew up under the fostering care of the Constitution itself; if it is a crime it is one that the South has incontrovertibly inherited from the founders of the republic; if the world has awakened to a sense of its inhumanity and immorality the Government should not have lost sight of its obligations in the matter, but should have sought to eliminate the evil by correct and honorable business methods."

"Syranus," said Joe, "suppose Mr. Lincoln, immediately after his election or before the Southern States began to secede, had announced that as his policy, that is, to have the Government pay the South a fair sum for the slaves and then set them free, do you think the South would have accepted the offer?"

"I do not," said Syranus; "the Southern States were then and are now contending for a principle rather than an institution – the right to control their own affairs in accordance with and under the guarantees of the Constitution. But I do believe that Mr. Lincoln would thereby have made a favorable impression on the Southern people, and probably have prevented the secession of the Southern States. There was already intense opposition to secession throughout the South; most of the Southern States seceded by only small majorities, and I doubt not that Mr. Lincoln could have defeated it, at least in some instances, by the manifestation of such an unmistakable evidence of fairness to the South.

"I may be unduly prejudiced in the matter, but it is hard for me to reconcile his failure to do so with his undoubted good judgment, independence of thought and action, sense of fair play, and great good nature."

The Confederate Army Starts For Tennessee

At the close of the "hundred-days fight" the Federal Army, under General Sherman, had possession of Atlanta, while the Confederate Army, now under General Hood, toil-worn and battle-scarred, was lying near Jonesborough, just south of Atlanta. On September 18, 1864, General Hood's army left that place, and started on the long march into Tennessee. Soon after that General Sherman's army started on what is called "The march to the sea." Thus the two armies moved off in nearly opposite directions. By that time the South had put in service all its available men; indeed, as General Grant said, it had "robbed the cradle and the grave" to strengthen its armies. So General Sherman in his march to the sea had little more to dispute his way than defenseless old men, women and children.

The route of the Confederate Army led across northern Georgia, thence across northern Alabama, and thence into Tennessee, crossing the Tennessee River on a pontoon bridge near Florence. The army passed through the battle ground of New Hope Church and the sites of other battles of the "hundred-days fight." These scenes of conflict were now sad sights. When the battles were fought, mostly in June and July, the trees were covered with green leaves; but nearly all the trees, large and small, were killed by musket and cannon balls in the fierce combats; so that the once lovely forests now looked like old deadenings; they were still covered with foliage, but it was brown and crisp. Not a cow, hog, chicken, or even a bird could be seen. Scattering stalks of green corn, oats and barley were growing in the woods from seeds dropped by the armies in feeding the stock. These green plants, so attractive under normal conditions, were here silent mementos of the ravages of war.

One beautiful afternoon the army pitched camp near the Etowah River The water was clear, and sang with a sweet murmur as it flowed between its clean and pebble-lined banks. Several of the men went to the river with their canteens to get a supply of water for the night. Nick was in the party, and as he neared the stream he saw something floating in the water which he thought might be valuable. It had lodged against a large rock in the middle of the river. Quietly but quickly his coat and shoes were "shucked off," and before the others knew what he was up to, he plunged into the chilly water and swam to the rock. Climbing up on it and walking to its upper end, he stooped and lifted from the water a first-class hickory shirt. What a glorious find! In an ecstasy of joy he waved it above his head, and there is no telling how much he was envied by the men who were watching him from the shore. Nick wore that shirt into Tennessee, and afterwards into North Carolina.

Nick, on returning to his comrades, said, "Boys, when I was on that rock I looked across the river and saw many pumpkins in the field on the other side."

That was another glorious find in which all the men were at once interested. It was soon known throughout camp, and nearly every man in the 12th made a rush for the river. They swam across, and each of them, I suppose, got one or more pumpkins. Their recrossing of the river with the pumpkins was the prettiest sight Nick saw during the war. As they swam they pushed the pumpkins ahead of them or held them by their stems with their teeth, and all were as gay and sportive as if they had been on a picnic. That evening the camp kettle was brought into use, and the Dixie boys had a great feast in which the only dishes were "cush" and boiled pumpkin, and these were seasoned only with salt and red pepper.

A Student-Soldier

If this story has a moral it is that a lad who has the will can learn much without a teacher, and that too under the most adverse circumstances. However, one may not be entitled to much credit for perseverance expended in pursuit of a subject that he really likes. When Nick left college for the war his class was just finishing the sophomore year, and therefore had not reached the higher mathematics – analytics and calculus. In the subjects passed over, arithmetic, algebra, geometry, and trigonometry, Nick was quite thorough, owing to a liking rather than a talent for mathematics, though wise men tell us that the former is some evidence of the latter.

In addition to Nick's fondness for the subject he had a consuming desire to see what lay beyond the boundaries of his attainments. The attempt to satisfy this desire occupied his mind, if not his time, during the war more than all the affairs of camp and field. When not actively engaged on duty he found delight in poring over some problem or theorem of real or imaginative entities. Speaking of him Joe[10] said, "He swims around most of the time in a sea of formulas."

Nick formed such a liking for tactics that he obtained a copy of Hardee's textbook on the subject, which was then in use, and made a study of it. The result was that he was often detailed to drill squads and companies. Having been elected second sergeant of his company, and finding that the duties were such as to allow him more or less time for study, he retained that office throughout the war.

At some old secondhand bookstore Nick obtained a copy each of Davies's *Analytic Geometry* and *Differential and Integral Calculus*, packed them from place to place, and entered into their wonderful unfoldings with no less of diligence than delight. Such was his progress in these and other subjects that at the close

---

10. Maj. J.W. Boring, Longview, Tex.

of the war Homer College tendered him the chair of mathematics, and conferred on him the degree of Master of Arts. Subsequently he prepared textbooks on calculus and trigonometry which were adopted, respectively, by Yale and Harvard.

Of course it would be out of place in a sketch like this to notice in detail Nick's achievements in various kinds of mathematical work and research. The point is not that he did so much but that he accomplished what he did without a teacher and almost without the aid of books. Among the interesting formulas which he deduced is the following singular value of the ratio of the circumference of a circle to the diameter:

$$\pi = 2(1-1)^{1/2}(1-1)^{-1/2}$$

Many years after the war the proof of this formula was given in a mathematical magazine published at Des Moines, Iowa, edited by Dr. J.E. Hendricks.

Nick's "musical circle" will probably be of interest to a much wider circle of readers. Some of the young men of the regiment organized a brass band and Nick joined it largely for the purpose of studying the science of music. He believed, and still believes, that the laws of music can be "harnessed in and by mathematical formulas" pretty much as the laws of projectiles and electricity are. In this undertaking he was led to the discovery, among other things, of the following simple mnemonic device for remembering the order of the sharps, the flats, and keys. This little artifice is now published for the first time, fifty years after its discovery.

Draw a circle, and divide the circumference into seven equal parts. Begin at any point of division and write *A*, and at the the alternate points write in order, *B*, *C*, *D*, *E*, *F*, *G*. This arrangement gives at once:

(1) The order of the sharps, *F, C, G, D, A, E, B.*
(2) The keys by sharps, *G, D, A, E, B, F, C.*
(3) The order of the flats, *B, E, A, D, G, C, F.*
(4) The keys by flats, *F, B, E, A, D, G, C.*

A Perilous Adventure

A long time ago, in a humble home in the great city of New York, was born a boy named Robert.[11] Henry Ward Beecher said, "There is no telling what is wrapped up in a boy's jacket." This might well have been applied to Robert, though he, like many other heroic souls, has never attained great wealth or high station in civil life.

When quite a young man he came to the South, and, like many other good and brave men of the North, became one of the Dixie people. When the Civil War broke out he was among the first to enlist in the Confederate Army. He began as a private but soon became a captain. He was in the siege at Port Hudson; that is, he was with the Dixie soldiers who were hemmed in there by the Federal soldiers, so that they (the Dixie boys) could get no more food from, and have no conference with, their friends on the outside.

Now Robert told the Dixie leader, General Gardner, that he would carry a message from him to General Johnston, the Dixie leader on the outside, although several men had already tried to do so, and had been killed or captured on the way. The general wrote the message, gave it to Robert, and said, "Good-by. God bless you."

---

11. Maj. R.L. Pruyn, Baton Rouge, La.

The Mississippi River flows by Port Hudson, and is 1200 yards wide there. Robert knew the country well, as it was not far from his home. His plan was to swim the river and land at a point about fifteen miles below, because the bank opposite Port Hudson was guarded by Federal sentinels. One night about nine o'clock, with five canteens buckled around his waist, he waded into the water and began his long swim.

The swim was not only a long but a perilous one. The river was lined with Federal gunboats and its banks with Federal pickets; the route led through many eddies and cross-currents of the great river; the long stay in the water was likely to produce cramps; and the peril was increased by his having to swim in his clothes. He reached his landing place about four o'clock the next morning, his swim having lasted about seven hours. He delivered the message to General Johnston at Jackson, Mississippi, and then took a message from General Johnston back to General Gardner.

In returning, Robert crossed the river in a horse trough a few miles above Port Hudson, and went down the western bank to a point just opposite Port Hudson. There he waited in the bushes until the sentinels were posted on the levee. He thus learned their positions. And so, after dark, he passed unseen between two of them, and, reaching the river, swam across into Port Hudson. Both the officers, Johnson and Gardner, spoke in high praise of his conduct.[12]

---

12. On the Boulevard at Baton Rouge is a Confederate monument. Here the local ex-Confederates often assemble to tell anew the stories of the past. Prominent in this assembly is Robert, respected and esteemed in his old age by all who know him.

General Sherman and Colonel Boyd

The Louisiana State University, now domiciled at Baton Rouge, had its origin in the Louisiana State Seminary and Military Academy, which was located in the piny woods near Alexandria, Louisiana. This embryo of the university began its career January 2, 1860, with William Tecumseh Sherman as Superintendent, and David French Boyd as Professor of Ancient Languages. Colonel Sherman was an Ohioan and a graduate of West Point; and Professor Boyd was a native of Virginia, and a graduate of her great university. Between these two men, who had so many like qualities of heart and mind, there sprang up at once a mutual admiration, which ripened into a friendship that strengthened with the lapse of years.

Pending the growing estrangement between the North and the South, which culminated in the secession of the Southern States in 1861, Colonel Sherman frankly and firmly sided with the North, and when Louisiana seceded he at once resigned the superintendency of the Seminary, went North, tendered his services to President Lincoln, and became one of the greatest generals of the Civil War.

Professor Boyd espoused the cause of the South, and was among the first to enlist in her military service. During the first two years of the war he served gallantly in the Army of Virginia. He was then transferred to the Trans-Mississippi Department and assigned to the corps of engineers under General Taylor, with the rank of major.

In the dense woods near Alexandria, while running some contour lines, Major Boyd was seized by a band of jayhawkers.[13] As they hurried him along to their secluded retreat they debated as to what disposition they would make of him. The majority favored "putting him out of the way," but some advocated turning him over to the "Yankees" in exchange for coffee and sugar. Before deciding the matter they reached Black River, and while crossing the stream their skiff capsized, and one of the guerrillas would have been drowned had it not been for the help of Major

---

13. Guerrillas.

Boyd. This kind act of the prisoner caused the captors to decide upon carrying him to the Federals at Vidalia, Louisiana.

Then followed a long and toilsome tramp across the swamp of the great river. The jayhawkers, fearing encounters with citizens and Confederate scouts, traveled mostly in the deep woods or along bypaths which led through solitudes unrelieved by the faintest trace of man. Major Boyd had a fine and irrepressible sense of humor, and never was it a greater support to him than on this trying occasion. He was, as it were, the one cheerful spirit in a mourning household. Arriving finally at Vidalia he was turned over to the Federals, the inference being that he was bartered for coffee and sugar. His quarters were established in the local jail pending his transference to some Northern prison.

In the meantime General Sherman, now high in rank and in the councils of his country, came along on a tour of inspection, and hearing of the fate of the major had him escorted to his office. When they met smiles broke suddenly like beams of light on their faces. Each realized, as probably never before, that there are ties which even war cannot sever.

At that time Confederate prisoners were exchangeable or not according to certain local conditions, not necessary to explain here. General Sherman, in order to get the major on the exchangeable list, determined to take him to New Orleans and turn him over to General Banks. So he had the major to take passage with him on his boat, and on the trip down the river treated him as his honored guest, providing him with a stateroom and having him to dine at the same table with himself. After a short confinement in prison at New Orleans the major was exchanged and at once returned to his duties under General Taylor.

Soon after the war Major Boyd was elected superintendent of the Seminary, which position carried with it the rank of colonel in the State militia. The rest of this story, though important as to the facts related, will probably be most interesting to the general reader by its disclosure of General Sherman's continued regard for the institution and its new president.

In 1869 the buildings of the Seminary were destroyed by fire, and the institution was removed to Baton Rouge, and temporarily housed in a part of the large edifice erected by the State for the care and education of its deaf and dumb. In 1874 Colonel Boyd, on the recommendation of General Sherman, was appointed superintendent of the Khedivial Military Academy, Cairo, Egypt. This position the colonel declined chiefly on account of his aversion to severing his connection with the school intrusted to his care, although at that time the institution was literally perishing for want of the support of the "carpetbag" State government, and also of the impoverished people struggling under its untold evils and abuses.

General Sherman became commander of the army in 1869, which position he resigned in 1884. In 1879, while passing through the South looking after military conditions, he stopped ov-er at Baton Rouge, and for the time was the guest of the institution into which the Seminary expanded on the decline of the carpetbaggers: namely, the Louisiana State University. A banquet was tendered him by the school in which, using the language of the general, many "gallant men who wore the gray" cheerfully participated.

Lying along the north boundary of the city of Baton Rouge is a stretch of land containing 210 acres, with a high bluff-front of 600 yards overlooking the Mississippi River. This beautiful and valuable tract is now the home and property of the university, and no more appropriate site for a great school is imaginable. When one surveys it, one is equally attracted by its beauty, its healthfulness, its value, and its interesting and romantic history. It is ideal for pleasure and meditation. The imagination is touched and kindled by the thousand stirring associations which hover over it. Here played the mighty forces which molded the civilization of the Southwest, and here Louisiana laid the foundation of her future greatness and power. A typical Louisiana spot – carpeted with a living green and lulled by the ceaseless murmur of the Father of Waters – fields of corn and rice, cotton and sugar cane stretch out around it, gulf breezes sweep over it, and the dark shadows of the live oak and magnolia fall across it. How the university came by this splendid property is as naturally asked as it is briefly answered.

Attracted by its elevation and commanding position, Bienville established a military post here soon after the founding of New Orleans (1718). Under the successive dominations of the French, Spaniards, and Americans the post was continued, improved, and expanded into a strong garrison with massive buildings for supplies, officers, and men. At one time or another nearly all the noted soldiers of the nation were stationed here. It was the home of General Taylor when he was elected President of the United States. Beneath the splendid oaks listening crowds of citizens and soldiers have hung with rapture on the lips of the nation's great statesmen and orators.

In the course of time the conditions which made it advisable to found and maintain a military post at Baton Rouge ceased to exist, and in 1878 the Government discontinued the garrison. General Sherman, ever thoughtful of the school away down in Dixie which he helped so much to establish, recommended that the property be turned over to that institution. This proposition was warmly seconded and persistently pushed by the Louisiana delegation in Congress. In 1884 a bill, introduced by Hon. A.B. Irion, was passed giving the university the use of the grounds and buildings, and in 1902 a bill, introduced by Hon. S.M. Robertson, was passed making a complete donation of the property to the university for all time.

General Sherman died in 1891 and Colonel Boyd in 1899. Though dead, yet at "L.S.U." they still live. A beautiful memorial hall, erected by the alumni of the university in memory of David French Boyd, adorns the grounds; and in the assembly hall, side by side with those of Robert E. Lee and Stonewall Jackson, hangs a life-size portrait of William Tecumseh Sherman.[14]

---

14. The present President of the university is Col. Thos. D. Boyd, a younger brother of Col. D. F. Boyd, and under his able administration the institution has had a remarkable growth every way – in buildings, equipments, and attendance; in colleges of arts and sciences, agriculture, and engineering.

CHAPTER EIGHT
The Story of the Close of the War

Cheerful Endurance

In a speech just before the war a secessionist said, "The South can whip the North with popguns." Just after the war the speaker was derisively reminded of his boast. Not in the least abashed the old stager replied: "We could have done it, but they wouldn't fight us that way."

A Georgian, returning from the war, consoled himself with this reflection: "I am going home now and make a crop; as for the war I'm satisfied – I killed as many of them as they did of me."

On his way home after the surrender a "Johnnie Reb" (Confederate) fell in with a "Bobby Link" (Federal), and they were having a "high old lark" together.

"Johnnie," said Bobby; "we licked you."

"You didn't," said Johnnie; "we jes wore ourselves out er licking you."

Probably no part of the Civil War is more interesting, and certainly none is more pathetic, than the surrender of the Confederate Army and the return of the warworn veterans to their distant and desolate homes. The Dixie boys' capacity for cheerful endurance, which had been their mainstay in the toils and privations of camp and field, was now the one bright star in the rayless night settling over the Southern States.

Every resource of the South had been taxed to the point

of exhaustion. With her 600,000 men she had met the 2,750,000 of the North, fought over every foot of her soil, and protracted the struggle until more than half her forces were slain, disabled, or imprisoned. Many sections of Dixie, having been tramped over by both armies and swept by fire and sword for four years, might now answer to Sheridan's description of the Shenandoah Valley: "The crow that flies over it must carry his rations with him."

Yet when the end came the men stacked their guns in sadness but not in tears or bitterness. Returning to their homes they found their houses in ruins, their farms destroyed, their slaves freed, their stock killed, and their yards and gardens overgrown with weeds. What then and there occurred is well told by the eloquent Grady: "What does he do – this hero in gray with a heart of gold? Does he sit down in sullenness and despair? Not for a day. The soldier stepped from the trenches into the furrow; horses that had charged Federal guns marched before the plow, and fields that ran red with human blood in April were green with the harvest in June. Cheerfulness and frankness sweetened the energy which made bricks without straw and spread splendor amid the ashes of their war-wasted homes."

Closing Scenes

The last battle in which the 12th took part was the one at

Bentonville, North Carolina (March 20, 1865). On the retreat from there it passed through Raleigh, and here the men heard of the surrender of General Lee (April 9, 1865). A deep gloom like an ominous cloud fell on the troops – they had reached the climax of "the ever deepening tragedy of war." Legweary and footsore they plodded on toward Greensboro. Their sad plight was the more touching because of their tattered garb and empty haversacks.

Never did the men stand in greater need of reanimation; and with the want there came, as usual, "the doctor." This time it was the Reverend Mr. Pepper, Presbyterian chaplain of a Mississippi regiment. Everybody loved "Brother Pepper" because of his helpfulness, wit, gaiety, and goodness. He had somewhere picked up what appeared to be the skeleton of an old swaybacked horse. This animal's neck and back formed a deep concave arc, the highest points being his ears and the root of his tail. The regiment having stopped for a short rest, the men were lying on the grass by the road side when Brother Pepper came along on old "Traveler," without saddle or bridle.

At once a regular fusillade poured on him from the ranks.

"Hello, parson, how did you make the raise?"

"Say, Brother Pepper, is that a horse or a kangaroo? Come out of that fork, old man, I know you are in there, because I see your feet."

"Look here, Brother Pepper, is that the war horse you're going to charge 'em on?"

"Gentlemen," said the preacher, "one question at a time, if you please."

"Brother Pepper, what I'd like to know is this, how much is passage?"

"Now, Jim,"[1] replied the chaplain, "if you are really tired of walking, and will give me a dollar for my services, I'll teach you how to pace."

Nick, having served in the Army of Tennessee, never saw General Lee, yet felt as if he knew him personally. How many times had he been cheered by the news, "Lee has whipped 'em again." In every camp and home of Dixie during the war the main theme of conversation and the chief object of adoration, was "Mars Robert." Never was a man more idolized by soldiers and citizens. Their confidence in him as a commander and their esteem for him as a man were boundless. With them, as so graphically stated by Hon. Benjamin Hill: "He possessed every virtue of other commanders without their vices – a foe without hate, a soldier without cruelty, a victor without oppression, and a victim without murmuring; – as gentle as a woman in life, and grand in battle as Achilles."

In a word, he was the ideal of the South; and while this is high praise of him it is none the less eulogistic of the people of Dixie, for a real artist is an artist only to those who are themselves more or less artists. They must have had something of the same high elements of character.

To this may be ascribed the achievements so forcibly and classically described by the gifted Thomas Nelson Page:

"The South produced a people whose heroic fight against the forces of the world has enriched the annals of the human race, and whose fortitude in defeat has been more splendid than their valor in war."

The 12th belonged to that part of the Army of Tennessee

---

1. James Bernard.

which was surrendered at Greensboro, North Carolina, April 26, 1865. The capitulation of these two main armies of the South brought the war to a close. What battles had been fought! What thousands had been slain! What countless sums had been expended! The deeds of heroism on both sides have probably never been surpassed in all the annals of warfare. Surely both sides thought they had something to fight for.

What was it all about? Something smacking of real intelligence and patriotism now warns the writer to be careful what he says. There is such a thing as "the pot calling the kettle black." Few have been the quarrels in this world in which both parties were not to some extent blamable. The kind of man that makes one ashamed of the national melting pot is he who "searches the Bible for passages which may be interpreted as sure damnation for his enemies and sure glory for himself." "Charity is the first breath of real heaven that men and women feel here on earth."

They were all Americans – the products of our republican ideals and institutions – and all "fought for the right as God gave them to see the right." The valor, fortitude, and disinterestedness of both sides is the glorious heritage of the American people. That from which we should draw the greatest hope and promise, and in which we should feel the greatest pride and pleasure, is the assurance that Americans, North and South, are formed of the clay out of which the best soldiers and citizens are fashioned by the hands of the Great Potter.

In the fullness of time there may be erected in Washington, District of Columbia, a joint monument to Grant and Lee, built by the free offerings of the people of all sections of our great country and in appreciation of the splendid products of our republican institutions. So mote it be.

The Fortunes of an Old Flag

Anyone who has served in an army that has fought many battles and borne many hardships knows how much the men come to prize and love their flag. With them it is a companion that has shared their joys and sorrows, cheered them in the sunshine of triumph, and consoled them in the shadows of adversity.

It is prized by them, not merely as the emblem of their country, but also as a member of the family, and the more so if the men and the flag have grown old together in the service and are alike weather-stained and battle-scarred.

That the men of the 12th had this feeling for their flag is shown by the following incident. When it became known that the regiment was to be surrendered, Leon,[2] the adjutant, began to devise some plan by which the dear old flag might be kept from falling into the hands of strangers. He mentioned the matter to a few of his friends, one of whom was Nick.

The interest of the men was at once awakened, and they began to suggest ways by which it could be done. The following will show the plan agreed upon. That night they went quietly, one by one, to a nearby woodland; and, having concealed themselves in a dense copse, they took off Leon's clothes, and wrapped wrapped and pinned the flag closely around his body. Leon was a thin bony fellow and did not look unduly large when he put his clothes on over the flag. The next day the regiment was surrendered, but the flag could nowhere be found. The colonel (Graham) was much incensed, but his threats and appeals were alike unavailing. Leon thus carried the flag to his distant home in Bastrop, Louisiana, where he guarded and preserved it for many, many years. In the course of time the Memorial Hall in New Orleans was built for the preservation of just such relics. To this beautiful hall Leon consigned the flag, and there it has been ever since. The sequel of this story may not be uninteresting:

Forty-two years after the surrender, when Hon. N.C.

---

2. Capt. Leon Polk, Bastrop, La.

Blanchard was governor of Louisiana, the flags captured from the Confederates were returned to the several Southern States. Extensive preparations were made in New Orleans for the reception of these now mute emblems of American valor and good will. The governor was to be present and receive the flags in behalf of the State. It so happened at the last moment that he could not go, and he asked Nick to go in his place.

In the presence of a large assembly in Memorial Hall, Nick took the flags, one at a time, from the box in which they had been carefully packed and shipped, and read their descriptions as given by the adjutant general. Great applause followed each announcement, and continued as the curator bore the flag to its assigned position. Thus, as Nick said, "In this Southern Pantheon they have taken their places in the silent assembly over which hover the legends and story of Dixie, its ideals and its chivalry."

"In conclusion," said he, "for one reason it is well that the governor asked me to represent him on this occasion, and that one reason makes my presence here somewhat of a coincidence. You have probably noticed that the flag of the 12th regiment was 'not present or accounted for' in this consignment. It so happens that I can explain the cause of its absence."

Then he pointed to the old flag in question and told its interesting history.

The Curtain Falls on a Scene Both Sad and Droll

Of the one thousand two hundred men that had belonged to the 12th from first to last only about one hundred seventy-five were left to be surrendered, and many of these were sick, feeble, or maimed. It soon became known that the surgeon would examine the men and report such as were unable to walk to their far-away homes in Louisiana. These were to be given transportation by rail, and all the others – the strong and healthy – would have "to foot it."

"Nick," said Oat, "I believe I'm taking the rheumatism."

"Why," asked Nick, "do you select rheumatism instead of some other disease?"

"Because," said Oat, "the doctor can't tell from a fellow's

pulse, or tongue, or temperature whether he is lying or not."

Oat's purpose was to have some fun as well as to get a long ride.

When the drum beat for the sick to fall in for the examination, Oat, with one leg bent at the knee and one arm at the elbow, hobbled along on a stout stick as if in great pain. He took his place in the long line of men enfeebled by disease or bullets. Tottering in weakness and in rags these grim warriors of many a well-fought field were pitiable to behold, and, as the surgeon drew near, the most forlorn phenomenon of the whole line was Oat.

On reaching Oat the surgeon asked, "What is the matter with you?"

"Got the rheumatism," said Oat.

"Where is it located?" inquired the doctor.

"Mostly in my joints, but there is also a pain in my back as long and wide as the blade of a saw."

He played the role so cleverly that he obtained a pass to ride, and so comically that it put the whole camp to laughing, and thus changed the gloomy occasion into a very pleasant affair.

To show how poor were the means for traveling by rail we will run ahead of our story, and relate a strange coincidence.

Among those who secured permits to go by rail on account of disabilities were Mark[3] and William,[4] and these were home-neighbors of Nick. On May 2, Nick, in bidding them goodbye, said, "Tell my people I am well, and will get home sometime."

One month afterwards, June 2, Nick and his party, on their way home, were ascending the Mississippi River, riding on the hurricane-deck of a steamboat. On reaching the mouth of Red River Nick remarked, "See, Mac, our boat, instead of turning into the Red, seems to be going to the Mississippi side." Mac, looking ahead, saw two men standing on the Mississippi shore, and replied, "I reckon she is going over to take those two fellows aboard." Sure enough, the boat landed, and as the two men started aboard Nick exclaimed, "Look, Mac, 'for the life of me,' it is Mark and William. What a singular coincidence!"

Such was the condition of the railroads that it took Mark and William one month to go from Greensboro to Vicksburg. At that time the river was very high, and, the levees being destroyed, the entire Mississippi bottom was buried beneath a great overflow. So the two wayfarers could reach home from Vicksburg only by descending the Mississippi River and ascending the Red. They arrived at the Red just in time to catch the boat on which was their regiment.

There are probably few other instances in which pedestrians kept pace with railroad trains for a distance of a thousand miles.

---

3. Dr. M. A. Taylor, Honey Grove, Tex.
4. Wm. Martin, Sherman, Tex.

CHAPTER NINE
The Story of the Homeward Tramp
☆ ☆ ☆ ☆

The Remnant Starts Home

When those on the "sick list" had been given passes there were left in the 12th about seventy well men who had to make their way home as best they could. They regarded the long tramp with less aversion than one would at first imagine. "They had been schooled," as Joe said, "in toils and hardships until they could walk like horses, endure like oxen, and sleep anywhere that alligators could." Furthermore, they would have no loads to carry except an old blanket apiece, and, being free from military restraints, could go as they pleased.

On the third day of May they turned their faces westward, Nick being one of the party, and with only $1.10 apiece (their part of the Confederate treasury) they started on the long journey across North Carolina, South Carolina, Georgia, Alabama, Mississippi, and into Louisiana. As a rule they traveled about thirty miles per day. Their movements showed a striking example of the force of habit. So accustomed were they to marching in order, that, no matter how they started, they would soon be walking with the step in files of twos or fours.

Their chief want was something to eat. It was probably Tom[1] who described them as being "too poor to buy, too proud to beg, and too honest to steal." So they were in a bad fix. How-

---

1. Hon. A. T. Nelson, Homer, La.

ever, the Federal provost marshals in the larger towns issued them "small rations of hardtack and pickled pork." The ladies along the way were always anxious to help them, but they were often as destitute as the soldiers themselves. Every place bore mute but eloquent testimony to the ravages of war. Often the fields and gardens were destroyed, and not a cow, hog, or chicken could be seen about the wasted homes. Fortunately, black berries were ripening along the roadside, and these helped to allay the pangs of hunger.

A Great Southern Leader

Their route is indicated by the following towns, through which they passed: Salisbury and Charlotte, North Carolina, Union and Abbeville, South Carolina, Atlanta and LaGrange, Georgia, and Opelika and Montgomery, Alabama.

Near Abbeville they loitered for some time about the boyhood home of John C. Calhoun. A halo of memories seemed to hover over and illumine every spot on which the boy once romped, laughed, and mused. Amid the reflections suggested by these scenes one is reminded of the large number of great men who were reared in the country. Washington, Jefferson, and Madison, Calhoun, Clay and Webster, Lincoln, Davis, and Lee, and many other truly great men were country-raised boys. Behind the simple and potential strength of all these men lay the forces which were molded in youth by the toils and lessons, tonics and inspirations, of country life.

Although Nick (or rather his people) did not belong to the political party of which Calhoun was the leader and the exponent, nor wholly indorsed his views of slavery, yet no one surpassed Nick in appreciation of the mental force and moral integrity of the great South Carolinian. As Mr. Davis says, "His prophetic warnings speak from the grave with the wisdom of inspiration." It was a beautiful tribute paid him by Daniel Webster, his greatest political rival, though his personal friend: "There was nothing groveling, or low, or meanly selfish, that came near the head or the heart of Mr. Calhoun."

Probably the most memorable event in the life of Calhoun was the debate between him and Webster on the character of the Federal Government. What many of the thoughtful and conservative men of the South thought of that debate and of the two participants is briefly expressed in the following extract from an address delivered by Nick in 1912 on the occasion of the Commencement Exercises of the Louisiana State Normal School. The speaker in discussing the function and potentiality of the imagination, and the importance of training it, said:

"The great historian is not he who merely garners the facts and statistics of the past and presents them in a logical and chronological order, but he who takes these facts and by an exuberant and constructive imagination breathes into them the breath of life. He reproduces the motives and spirit of the past and transports the reader into its joys and its sorrows. He not only articulates its dry bones, but he puts flesh upon them and sends the warm blood coursing through the veins.

"We need not revert to other times or climes for a striking instance of the potentiality of a trained and constructive imagination. We have one in the history of our own country. Calhoun and Webster were great orators and statesmen. Calhoun excelled in logic and Webster in imagination. The memorable debate between these two intellectual giants on the character of the Federal Government shook the nation from center to circumference. It was a battle royal between facts fortified by logic on the one side and facts vitalized by imagination on the other. Thirty years thereafter the issue was decided by the arbitrament of battle, and logic went down under the onward sweep of imagination."

An Old-Time Southern Aristocrat

Having strolled on ahead of the rest of the party Nick crossed the Savannah River all alone, and immediately left the

Hill Memorial Library

View of part of the campus of Louisiana State University.

main road in search of food. Really he had learned what it is to be hungry. How different is the ordinary craving for food from that produced by months of poor and insufficient nutriment. To persons who have felt only the former, the "pangs of hunger" are utterly meaningless words. Hunger such as the Confederates often endured, is, as Eggleston says, "the great, despairing cry of a wasting body – an agony of the whole body and soul as well."

Nick approached a dwelling which had evidently seen better days. It appeared to be deserted except by the swallows that fluttered about the old weather-stained columns. In response to his "hello" a venerable old lady came out on the front gallery. She wore a home spun dress and a frilled cap. In her face and bearing there was something familiar to Nick – an expression that he had known. "Probably," thought he, "I have seen her before." No; what he recognized was merely the common mark of a typical Southern woman of the upper class.

She was a so-called "Southern Aristocrat." But Nick knew, and all her neighbors knew, that her aristocracy was one of nobility rather than of wealth, fortune, and rank. From that home comfort and luxury might depart but the sweet ministrations of culture and refinement never. No one could approach her with undue familiarity, yet her intercourse with the prince and the pauper, the master and the slave, was marked by the gentlest courtesies. While she was proud, hers was a heart that could reach down to the suffering and hold poor little dying babes on her breast. In her face was a firmness which was as soft as velvet and yet as inflexible as steel. Her face had a haggard look, such a look as comes from toil, anxiety, and scanty food, but behind it all was a fortitude that toil could not chill nor privations shatter. Her husband and older sons had perished in battle, and the fruits of their toil and thrift were perishing around her; but for all that she bore herself with a brave composure. In the throes of impending disasters she might lose all, – might go to the stake or to penury, – but she would meet it supported by the serene and supreme conviction that she was a lady.

It was a part of her creed to consider no woman refined who does not naturally avoid the society of men; Nick knew this, but he also knew that she would not be unladylike even to a stranger or a beggar. Lifting his cap he approached her reverently but with the utmost freedom. Gently touching his hand she said, "My dear boy, you are hungry; come with me into the dining room." His clothes were ragged and his shoes tied together with strings; but that made no difference with her, provided only that he was a gentleman.

Arriving at the table she lifted an immaculate white cloth and thus uncovered a few pones of corn bread and two roasted squirrels. To these she helped Nick bountifully, but made no apology for the coarse and scanty fare. With a well-balanced mixture of mirth and sadness she chatted of current events, but not a word of her own troubles was spoken. Nor did she refer to a recent raid of some "Yankee plunderers" who had stripped her of her silverware and heirlooms.

As Nick was leaving she hailed a passing Negro and said to him kindly, "Henry, please show this gentleman the near way back to the main road." With his head bowed in reverence and meditation Nick walked slowly away. "I wonder," mused he, "if any country ever produced a nobler race of women than the South? For courage, fortitude, and high ideals they surely have never been surpassed. At home and in the hospital, in camp and on the battle field, their heroic, self-sacrificing, and merciful deeds during this terrible war will never be fully known 'until the angels make their report."

A Few Great Georgians

Amid the ruins of Atlanta, Hon. A. H. Stephens, ex-Vice President of the Confederacy, was strolling about under the escort of a Federal guard. He had just been arrested by order of the National Government, and was then being taken to trial for "treason" against his country. It was a sad and a ludicrous sight. Bodily he was so small he looked like a boy, and his guard so large that he looked like a giant. Nick was reminded by the scene of a rather noted incident that happened some years before the war.

On the occasion referred to, Stephens and Judge — were opposing speakers in some political controversy. The latter, being a very large man and wishing to discredit the former by making sport of his littleness, said, "If his head were greased and his ears pinned back I could swallow him."

"Probably you could," retorted the little man, "but if you did you would have more brains in your stomach than in your head."

Many of the people Nick had known, including his father and mother, were Georgians by birth, and a Georgian, wherever found, seldom tires of extolling the glories of the "Cracker State." Therefore, Nick had heard much of the "big men" of this grand old commonwealth, especially the "trio," Stephens, Hill, and Toombs. These, so thought and claimed many Georgians, were the peers of Clay, Calhoun, and Webster. In this, as in many other cases, there may be a difference between "Mirabeau judged by his friends and Mirabeau judged by the people." But waiving all invidious comparisons, there are few who will deny that, in the skill and power of oratory, in felicity of expression and exuberance of thought, in logic and imaginative force, the Georgia Trio was hard to beat.

Henry W. Grady, himself a later Georgian who "reached the high water mark of modern oratory," said:

"The wisest speech, and the ablest ever made by an American, in my opinion, is Mr. Toombs's speech on slavery, delivered in Boston about ten years before the war. In that speech he showed a prescience almost divine, and clad in the light of thirty years of confirmation, it is simply marvelous.

"Who saves his country, saves all things, and all things saved will bless him. Who lets his country die, lets all things die, and all things dying curse him."

In the city of Atlanta this literary gem is graven on the statue of its author, Benjamin H. Hill, and in the "garden of literature" there is probably not a richer fruit or a flower more beautiful.

Hill's tribute to Lee is no less a mosaic than an epic:

"He was Cesar, without his ambition; Frederick, without his tyranny; Napoleon, without his selfishness; and Washington, without his reward. He was a foe without hate, a friend without treachery, a soldier without cruelty, a victor without oppression, and a victim without murmuring."

In opposition to secession Stephens led the "unionists." In the midst of the momentous issues that confronted the people, the secessionists and unionists were earnestly looking for light to guide them in that hour of travail and uncertainty. By request, Mr. Toombs, a leading secessionist, addressed the General Assembly of Georgia one evening and Stephens addressed it the next (November 14, 1860.) Both delivered masterpieces of oratory. The following excerpts from the speech of the latter are no less important lessons to-day than when delivered:

Speaking of the benefits of the government under which we have lived and prospered Mr. Stephens said: "They are so silent and unseen that they are seldom thought of or appreciated. The influence of the government on us is like that of the atmosphere around us. We seldom think of the single element of oxygen in the air we breathe, and yet, let this simple, unseen, and unfelt agent be withdrawn, this life-giving element be taken away from this all-pervading fluid around us, and what instant and appalling changes would take place in all organic creation."

In illustrating how hard, if not impossible, it is to restore the civic virtues and institutions of a country when once they have been destroyed, he thus cited the case of Greece:

"Descendants of the same people inhabit the country; yet what a mighty difference. In the midst of present degradation we see the glorious fragments of ancient works of art – temples with ornaments and inscriptions that excite wonder and admiration, the remains of a once high order of civilization which have outlived the language they spoke. Upon them all Ichabod is written – their glory has departed. Why is this so? I answer thus, their institutions have been destroyed. These were but the fruits of their forms of government, the matrix from which their grand development sprung; and when once the institutions of our people shall have been destroyed, there is no earthly power that can bring back the Promethean spark to kindle them here again, any more than in that ancient land of eloquence, poetry, and song."

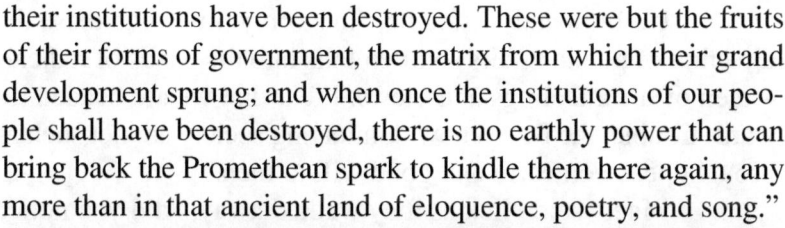

Like many other great men Stephens was simple and informal in his manners, and so freely did he intermingle with all classes that he was widely known as "the great commoner." Mac[2] and Nick greatly desired to see him at close range and hear him talk. Knowing how accessible he was they were emboldened to approach him, and, with permission of the guard, they did so, and were received with a smile, hearty handshakes, and "I am delighted to meet you."

There was something in his expression which bespoke anxiety and suffering, yet he talked cheerfully and soon put the boys at their ease. He asked them to tell him of their surrender, and drew from them much of the details of their long tramp from North Carolina to Georgia. As he laughed at the ludicrous descriptions of their ups and downs, Nick wondered how a man confronted with such serious concerns as he was could let his mind dwell on such light matters.

As to his own troubles – his impending trial and the result – he manifested but little solicitude, but of public ills he had grave

---

2. D. McD. Crow, Natchitouches, La.

forebodings.

Referring to the results of the war – the subversion of the industrial, economic, and social conditions and affairs of the South – "They are bound," said he, "to bring great hardships on the Southern people, and these will now be aggravated by the unfortunate death of Mr. Lincoln. Had he lived I doubt not that he, now that big main purpose of preserving the Union has been accomplished, would have sympathized with the South in her prostration and poverty, and sought to aid her in the readjustment of her affairs and in the rehabilitation of all the forces and agencies of peace and prosperity."

"Unfortunately," said he, "in stormy times like these the direction of public affairs so often falls into the hands of radicals – men of ultra feelings and views. I fear that we are headed towards trouble; the forces now dominating society are not such as brought peace on earth and good will to men.

"Mac," said Nick as they walked away, "did you notice how far above all petty spite and littleness he is?"

"Let me answer that question by asking another," said Mac. "Is that not always the case with one who has the courage of a soldier and the instincts of a gentleman?"

One of the many other fine characters of Georgia was General J.B. Gordon. Such was Nick's high appreciation of him that he named his firstborn son "Gordon."

"My dear young friend," once said the general to Nick, "while I thank you for the compliment, I would warn you to be careful about naming your sons after me and my folks. We are all Southern men of the old school."

"General," inquired Nick, "what is your idea of a man of that type?"

"Well," replied the general, "he won't lie nor he won't steal, but everything else will he do."

General Gordon was fond of a good story, and few surpassed him in the art of telling one. Entertaining a crowd one day he said:

"These Episcopal bishops are usually broad gauged fellows and have the saving grace of good humor. One of this kind was once traveling through the country and came upon a clever though illiterate farmer.

"'My friend,' asked the bishop, 'what church do you belong to?'

"'I'm 'piscopal,' said the farmer.

"'Who confirmed you?' inquired the bishop.

"'Han't never been er – 'firmed, that I'se heard of.'

"'Tell me, my dear sir, how you became an Episcopalian.'

"'Well, it was this way. Some friends in the city asked me to come to see 'em; I went, and while there we all went to meetin' at the 'Piscopal Church. The main thing I heard 'em say was this: We've been doin' er mighty sight er things which we hadn't ought er do, and we've been leavin' undone er mighty sight er things which we had ought er do; then I said to myself, that's me; and ever since then I've been a 'piscopal.'"

"I reckon," added the General, "we are all more or less 'piscopals."

Nick was reminded of this story and its moral quite recently in reading a good book in which he found this: "If we all faced the truth about things, instead of sheltering ourselves in deceptions, perhaps the world would begin to improve."

And also this: "What fakirs we are – if anyone confesses to us things not half as bad as what we ourselves do or think, how often do we set that one down as a living, breathing atrocity."

A Long and Jolly Ride

The extended tramp across the defunct Confederacy, so fraught as we have seen with toils and privations and clouded by the shadows of present and impending troubles, was not devoid of enjoyable scenes and experiences. One of the places ever remembered by the wayfarers as an "oasis in the desert" is Opelika, Alabama. Hearing of the hunger of these homewardbound boys, the ladies of that then small village hastily made a table of goods boxes, and on it spread such articles of food as their meager larders could supply. Placed in the shade of the oaks and surrounded by a bevy of charming women it was a pretty sight, such a one as the poor fellows had not seen in many a day. Never did men eat more heartily or ravenously. The ladies smiled as they watched the performance, and doubtless excused the boys for their want of politeness in not leaving a crumb or scarcely a bone on the table.

"It never rains that it doesn't pour," is sometimes as true of pleasures as of troubles. Immediately after the good breakfast came a long ride which was as unexpected as it was joyous and restful. On account of the devastations wrought by first one army and then by the other the railroad running through Opelika to to Montgomery had not been in use for some time. Parts of the track and many of the bridged were destroyed, and what remained of the track was in places nearly hidden by growing grass and weeds.

At Opelika one old rickety box car was left, and Nick, noticing that the roadbed had a considerable down grade, said, "Boys, let's put our coats and blankets in this car, shove her off, and take a ride." The suggestion was accepted with great hilarity.

In went the luggage and off went the car. When once well started on the downgrade it was propelled by the force of gravity; then the men leaped into and upon it. The further it went the greater was its speed, so that its momentum at the end of the downgrade carried it far up the next upgrade. The riders were in a fever of excitement. The episode thrilled them with delight and with suggestions and expectations of greater things.

At once it was agreed "to charter the train" for the rest of the trip, push it along at the upgrades and ride in it over the downgrades. Fortunately Opelika has a much greater elevation than Montgomery; knowing this, Nick exclaimed, "Boys, there is going to be more riding than pushing."

"Attention!" ordered Mac. "I move we elect Nick conductor." The motion having prevailed, Nick took charge and immediately issued General Order, No. 1:

I. The battalion will be formed into two equal squads; and the squads will go on duty alternately every half hour.

II. Sergeant Guthrie[3] is hereby appointed Adjutant; he will proceed at once to form the squads and put the caravan agoing.

Yielding to the united pushing of about twenty-five men the train rolled along slowly until it reached the next downgrade; then, with all hands aboard, it moved off as if imbued with life, singing faster and faster its cheerful song of "clat-er-te-rack, clat-er-te-rack" as it went diving through the deep cuts and sailing over the high embankments. It was a jolly affair, and what the car lacked of making as much noise as any other train was more than made up by the laughing and yelling of the "passengers."

There had been no traffic on this road for several weeks, and the people living along the quiet route, as one can well imagine, were startled by such an unusual racket and appalling uproar. They rushed out of houses and fields to see what it was, and having ascertained the cause enjoyed the frolic as much as the boys themselves. As the singular phenomenon, having "no pushee and no pullee," approached Loachapoka a crowd was seen gathering at the depot. Responding to a signal from the crowd the speed of the car was slackened, and in the midst of much cheering and waving of hats and handkerchiefs, the "train" rolled slowly up to the station. The boys were now standing on top of the car, and between them and the crowd there opened up a regular fusillade – not one of firearms, but of questions, answers, jokes, and ex-

---

3. Guthrie was the old hospital steward, and the only man in the party who had even the semblance of a watch.

pressions of good will.

Before leaving this pleasant place the travelers were informed of the destruction of the bridge over the river a few miles ahead of them. This timely warning probably saved their lives, for it was downgrade all the way from there to the river.

Many years after that event, Nick met an old man who lived in that locality. He (the old man) related the incident, and turning to Nick said, "By the way, it has just occurred to me that they were from your State, and no doubt you have heard of the event before."

"Yes, my friend," said Nick, "that was the only train of which I ever had the honor of being the conductor."

More Surprises

A few miles east of Montgomery is Mount Meigs, and near this little village "Company Q," as our happy-go-lucky wayfarers styled themselves, came upon a mulberry orchard. It appeared to contain several acres, and the trees bore a harvest of tempting ripe fruit. Never had the boys seen a cultivated crop of that kind before, and to them a special feature of the novelty was the varied colors of the berries.

But however attractive the scene to the eyes of that hungry crowd it was their stomachs that were most interested in the outlook. As a rule, they did not enter gardens without leave; but on that occasion the writer does not remember whether they obtained permission to invade the orchard or not. He does recall a statement by Tom[4] as they resumed their journey: "Boys, I loaded up to the guards, then put up the sideboards and took on nearly as much more."

---

4. T. McEachern, Shongaloo, La.

Another pleasant surprise of the trip happened at Montgomery. On applying to the Federal officer in charge at that place "Company Q" was given free passage on a boat down the Alabama River to Mobile. This was a great relief, as it promised to shorten the long tramp by several hundred miles. Although the passage would be on the hurricane deck it was better than tramping in hot weather through the dust and sand.

"Mac," said Nick, "some of these Yankees are right good fellows after all."

"Yes," replied Mac, "I reckon that, on the whole, they are just about as good and as bad as we are. It is hard to see ourselves as others see us."

"There is something harder to do than that, Mac, and that is to reason correctly and justly when one's interests and prejudices are involved."

B-O-O-M! The boat quivered and the glass rattled.

"What was that?" was asked by several in chorus.

"It was an explosion of some kind," said Tom,[5] "and it seemed to be at some point ahead of us, probably Mobile."

"Well," exclaimed Tom,[6] I am somewhat used to great noises, but that beats any I ever heard, not excepting the bursting of the "Lady Polk" at Columbus, Kentucky. My! That, certainly, was a golly-whopper. The earth trembled as if riven by an earthquake."

On arriving at Mobile it was learned that in moving the ammunition surrendered by General Taylor a loaded bomb was dropped, and its bursting resulted in the explosion of many tons of powder. All over the city sheds were shaken down and panes of glass crashed by the concussion, and many people were said to have been buried under the ruins.

The Gulf and Its Chief Tributary

He was a shrewd if not a wise man who said, "I don't often meet with disappointment, for the simple reason that I am

---

5. Hon. A.T. Nelson, Homer, La.

6. T. McEachern.

not such a fool as to expect much from people." This accords with the beatitude, "Blessed is the man who expects nothing, for he shall not be disappointed." Company Q, being thus blessed, was prepared for a cheerful acceptance of whatever fell to its lot, be it a comfort or a discomfort. This was nowhere more fully exemplified than in its voyage across the Gulf.

The Federal officer in charge readily gave the men an order for transportation by boat to New Orleans, and in doing so pleasantly remarked, "I am treating you fellows to a delightful sea voyage."

"For which we sincerely thank you," ventured Mac.

"When you go aboard," said he, "if you see cause to withdraw your thanks remember it is the best we can do to-day in the way of a boat. However," continued he with a broad smile on his frank face, "I guess it is good enough for you rebels."

Mac, seeing that he was chock-full of humor and believing that no man thus equipped can be very narrow or sensitive, retorted, "Captain, we now see it is not true, as we have long been led to believe, that a smile on a Yankee's face is so unfamiliar to his features that they don't know how to manage it." At which the captain and all his office crew joined the "rebels" in a prolonged and hearty laugh.

"That's a splendid fellow," said Tom,[7] as the boys walked away.

On boarding the vessel it was seen to be old and dilapidated; and worse still, the great explosion of the day before had blown off the top of one of the wheelhouses.

"Hello, Mac! How about the thanks?"

"They stand," said Mac. "This is far better than we're used to, and as for safety that officer is of the kind that would never send men where he would not go himself, I don't care if he is a Yankee."

As usual the "berth" assigned the fellows was the hurricane deck, "thus honoring us as preferred guests," said the witty Ben, "by putting us above everybody else." The big bell tapped,

---

7. T. J. Baker, Athens, La.

the great wheel began churning the water, and the old craft glided out to sea. As she got more and more under good headway the water spouted higher and higher through the top of the wheelhouse and poured right into the berth of Company Q.

"Boys," again spoke Ben, "that officer was even more thoughtful of our welfare than we supposed; he knew we all needed a good washing. Think of it, a salt water bath!"

Now and then brisk gales made violent onsets against the falling streams of water, and drove them in tiny jets or spray in every direction. However, here and there were places uninvaded by jet or spray, and in these dry spots the passengers huddled like cattle in the shade of a lone tree. Under such conditions the wanton expenditure of pent-up energy was bound to break loose. And at it they went – songs, jokes, pranks, and stunts of many descriptions. For hilarity, this water trip was unsurpassed even by the land trip on the "crazy train."

A Black waiter slipped away from below and came up to enjoy the show. He was at home "wid dese White boys," for he had romped with their kind on many a similar frolic. The boys "took him in" at once, for they also knew his kind. Sam Jones says: "Shooting at birds with blank cartridges is just about as amusing to the birds as to the boys." "Henry" was just the target the boys wanted for a good old time like they used to have around the "swimming hole"; and while the jokes were pretty rough on Henry, he would have been disappointed – positively aggrieved – had he not received just such a mark of distinguished consideration.

"Is yu all got enny good water fur to drink?" asked Henry.

"No," said a dozen voices.

"Den I'se gwine to fetch yu sum, but don't yu let dem gent'men down dar know 'bout it."

So Company Q was supplied with an abundance of fresh

cool water. As for food, the situation was thus told by Ben: "If we observed the same Godlike temperance in all things that we do in eating we might be canonized for saints."

The next morning a loud and long huzza rent the air as the dark line of the Louisiana shore rose above the sea. Eyes beamed with delight, and here and there a rough hand brushed off a tear trickling down a bronzed cheek. The party boarded the old Pontchartrain Railroad, along which the infant Nick had been carried just twenty years before. Ragged, hungry, and penniless, they landed in the heart of the great metropolis. Not knowing what else to do, they established "temporary quarters" in an old vacant cotton shed. But they were not long alone. The ladies, ever on the lookout for homeward bound Confederates, began moving in that direction, and they were not of the kind who are so much like men that men often forget what is due them as women.

Embarrassed by their own unsightly garb the first impulse of the men on seeing the ladies was to hide. While "fine feathers make fine birds," the reverse is not always true. Despite the aspects of ragamuffins, these boys were gentlemen born and bred. Those elegant ladies, having no less of bonhomie than refinement, put the men at ease. By their words and manners the boys came to feel that they were the more appreciated for the very hardships of which they bore ample testimony. They were shown to a lavatory, where they had the joy and privilege of bathing like gentlemen. Then followed a meal consisting of such articles of food as the ladies already had prepared. Throughout the war the women of New Orleans were widely known for their Spartan valor, trueness to the cause, and kindnesses to Confederate soldiers.

Early in the war, coffee was sometimes issued to the men. No company ever had more than one or two coffee mills, and of course these sooner or later became very dull. One Sunday morning Jim was sitting on a log trying to grind coffee on a worn-out machine.

To one of the men passing by he exclaimed, "Mat,[8] this

---

8. Mat. Haynes, Shongaloo, La.

is a very industrious mill."

"How do you make that out, Jim?"

"When it gets done with one grain it starts on another."

Likewise, Company Q, on boarding a boat to go up the river, might have said, "When we get done with one hurricane deck we start on another."

The old Mississippi again! What a train of memories the sight of it awakened! Much of the soldiering of these veterans had been spent on its banks. Of Columbus, Island No. 10, New Madrid, Fort Pillow, Memphis, Vicksburg, and Port Hudson they had feeling recollections – pleasant and unpleasant. At all these points they had seen their comrades struck down by bullets or disease. But recollections of the battle's roar and the funeral march were mollified by remembrances of many a frolic on land and in the water.

Up the Mississippi they went, thence up the Red and Ouachita Rivers into northern Louisiana. Here and there one, two, or more of them left the boat as they reached their respective landing places. With each departure there were cordial handshakes and many a "God bless you" uttered in broken voices and with tear-moistened eyes. Among the last to leave the boat was a party of about fifteen, including Nick, who landed at the old town of Trenton late in the afternoon. The place was about sixty miles from their homes, but this "short distance" was considered an easy two-days' walk.

The Home Stretch

In the piny woods twelve miles from Trenton is a beautiful branch, to which the crowd at once started, cheered by the prospects of a refreshing bath in its clear running water. The walk was strenuous, and after the bath they slept soundly on the green sward beneath the trees. With clean skins and empty stomachs their homeward tramp was resumed early in the morning. Near Douglas they halted, and while resting in the shade of an oak, Nick said:

"Boys, here we come to the parting of the ways. The

Forest Grove chaps – Mark[9] Tom,[10] William,[11] and I – will now leave the main road and take a short cut to our homes."

A shadow of sadness fell over "this last assembly," and for the time there was little talking, no joking, no hilarity. After a bit Mac flashed into the cloud of gloom a ray of light and cheer with the suggestion:

"Boys, let us now agree that when any one of us gets married all the others will be expected to attend, without further invitation."

The motion was received with cheers, and unanimously adopted; and in the months and years which followed Nick had the pleasure of seeing nearly every one of the party promoted from a celibate to a benedict. Many of the members of that "last assembly" have crossed over the abyss that separates time and eternity. Of the few still living are Tom,[12] Mat,[13] and Tom.[14]

The next day Nick's party reached the old Cane Ridge and Homer road – that along which Nick and Step had played a long time ago (see page 61). Near the cabin in which they had taken refuge from the storm, Nick lay down in the shade and stretched out his weary limbs on the soft grassy sward. On a bush near by a wren piped its old-time song, and perched on the knot of a tall dead pine a woodpecker beat a faultless long roll. "Jay, jay, jay!" chanted a blue jay in a great hickory tree, while the breeze-swept pines filled the air with a soft melody not unlike the hum of a swarming colony of bees. These notes of the

---

9. Dr. M. A. Taylor, Honey Grove, Tex.

10. T. J. Baker, Athens, La.

11. Wm. Martin, Sherman, Tex.

12. Hon. A. T. Nelson, Homer, La.

13. Mat. Haynes.

14. T. McEachern.

woods, so familiar to Nick in his boyhood days, started within him a responsive train of memories:

"Nowhere in all my ups and downs has life been so joyous, so blithe, and so worth while as amid the scenes along this road and the two old plantations it connects. They now hover over and envelop me like a delicate fragrance. The remembrance of other events may stir my heart, but the memory of these alone stirs my soul. Here all things that have been most important in my life had their beginning. When first I traveled this road my great desire was to see the new place; now the oldness of the same place appeals to me as the newness of it never did."

Continued he, "The glory of war! What a strange hallucination! Except for the toil, sacrifice, and suffering that men endure for an ideal it is a misnomer, misconception, mockery. How few of the struggling troops ever think of the ideals, how many know nothing of the great underlying causes. Reason! In the tenets and doings of war is a strange place to look for it. One might as well expect to find sweetness in a crowd of boys tussling for pennies. Often has a battle reminded me of the fight between the dogs and the cat (page 22). With little thought of ideals and causes, mastery was the end aimed at and the arts of primitive instincts the means employed. War settles only questions of might, and it is a sad commentary on civilization that quarrels between states and nations are not adjusted by arbitration."

It was the seventh day of June, 1865 – the thirty-fifth and last day of the long tramp – and a little after nightfall, that Nick walked up to the front gate of his dear old home. For many weary days the home folks had been watching for his coming. The bark of an old hound, now a stranger to the boy who had raised him, announced the arrival of the unknown. In a twinkling there was a rush in that direction from all quarters. Here came the Whites, the Blacks, and the dogs, each one making a racket of some character. In the midst of the uproar, with the arms of his three sisters about him, Nick heard Uncle Wash say, "My son! We are so glad to see you!" which, as Nick knew, was far for his father to go in the way of a demonstrative greeting.

The darkies politely stood aloof until the salutations of the

Whites had somewhat abated. Good Old Uncle Nathan, unable to restrain himself longer, burst in, and seizing Nick by the arms, exclaimed, "Bless de Lawd fur all his mercies; de boy is cum back to us er man." Aunt Callie, Nick's old nurse, came next, and grasping his hands she sobbed, "My dear baby boy! What fur you stay so long? Yo Callie ben waitin',watchrn', and prayin' fur yu all dese years. My! What a big un my baby is got to be!" To her hand Nick held fast for the very comfort to be had from that living contact. One by one he shook hands with all the darkies, though so many of the younger ones had grown out of his knowledge, he had often to ask who they were.

Later on, when the moon was creeping down behind the trees, Nick and his sister "Duck"[15] sat alone on the front gallery, and in reverie watched the gathering shadows. Each felt that, the other was thinking of her whose absence was the one great blank in the joy of Nick's home-coming.

"Brother," said the sister, "her anxiety for you and the other three boys wore out her sweet life. Oh, the saddest day I have ever known was that in which I followed her dear body to the cedars in the old churchyard."

Somewhere nearby a cricket chirped sadly "as if it were human and could understand." Likewise sang the katydids in an oak near the house.

To bring back the brightness which had gone out of things Nick went off on a new tack, "Sister, how about my sleeping to-

---

15. Mrs. J.W. Willis, Shreveport, La.

night? For a long time my bed has been a blanket spread on the ground with a chunk under one end of it for a pillow. Really I feel that one of that kind out there under the trees would be the most comfortable bed you could give me."

It was hard for him to convince her that he meant what he said. At last she said, "I wish you to sleep in the house; I can give you a hard mattress and a bolt of cottonade for a pillow."

Duck smiled, and Nick smiled when he saw her fixing his bed that way. With a sweet caress she bade him good night.

Nick stretched himself out on the hard, but to him comfortable, bed, and lay for a long time staring through the open window up into the night. The stars were shining as in the days long gone by, but all else, how changed. He closed his eyes and gradually memories of the loved and the lost sank to rest like the waves at sea when the storm is spent. "Something in his brain, which seemed to tick the slow movement of time, came suddenly to a stop like a clock that has run down," and Nick was asleep.

The End.

www.ingramcontent.com/pod-product-compliance
Lightning Source LLC
LaVergne TN
LVHW051100080426
835508LV00019B/1987